THE ACHIEVEMENT ALGORITHM

THE ACHIEVEMENT ALGORITHM

Cracking the Code
to Sustainable Leadership

Charlotte Fuller

authors
AND CO.

First published in Great Britain in 2025
by Authors & Co.
www.authorsandco.pub

ISBN 978-1-915771-49-0 (paperback)

CONTENTS

INTRODUCTION:

CRACKING THE CODE TO SUSTAINABLE LEADERSHIP

In today's fast-paced world, the pursuit of success often feels like a relentless race. Leaders, executives, entrepreneurs and high achievers are constantly pushing harder, driven by the belief that the only way to stay ahead is through sacrifice and never-ending hustle. We've been raised on the notion that hard work is the key to success but we're seldom told about the toll it takes on our mental, emotional and physical well-being. But what if that belief is flawed? What if there's a better way? What if you could achieve everything you want — career success, personal fulfilment and financial abundance — without burning out?

The formula for sustainable success exists and it's far more attainable than you might think. It's not just about working harder, and it certainly isn't about slapping on a smile and "thinking positively". It's about something deeper, something more strategic. Most importantly, it's grounded in science, practical wisdom and a new understanding of what it really takes to achieve at the highest level without the sacrifices we've been conditioned to accept. In this book, I'm going to show you exactly how to crack that code.

BEYOND POSITIVE THINKING: THE REALITY OF SUSTAINABLE SUCCESS

Let's be clear from the start: this book is not about superficial positive thinking or hoping that success will magically appear. It's not about writing affirmations on your mirror and waiting for things to fall into place. Yes, a positive mindset is essential, but it's just one piece of a much larger puzzle. Real, sustainable success requires a deliberate, holistic approach. This book introduces science-backed principles, proven strategies and a framework that enables you to achieve the kind of success that doesn't come at the cost of your health or happiness.

Through years of personal experience, research and coaching, I've learned that success is about **alignment** — aligning your thoughts, actions and beliefs with your deepest desires and true potential. When you achieve that alignment, everything begins to flow. You perform better, you feel better and success becomes a by-product of how you're living each day. The problem is that many of us have been taught to pursue success in a way that's misaligned. We believe that sacrifice, struggle and stress are necessary ingredients for achievement. But here's the truth: success doesn't have to be that hard. You don't need to sacrifice your well-being to reach your goals. The real secret lies in working with yourself, not against yourself.

MY JOURNEY: THE MOMENT IT ALL SHIFTED

I didn't always know this. Like many of you, I once believed that success was something you had to chase relentlessly. In my career as a management consultant, I was thriving on paper —I was travelling the world, leading major projects and working around the clock. By every conventional measure, I was successful. But beneath the surface, I was running on empty. My health was deteriorating, I was constantly stressed and no matter how much I achieved, it never felt like enough.

Then came the breaking point. My body simply couldn't keep up with the pace I had set for myself. I reached a point where everything collapsed – mentally, physically and emotionally. It wasn't just burnout; it was a complete shutdown. And while that moment was incredibly difficult, it was also the turning point in my life.

That forced pause led me to reassess everything I thought I knew about success. I realised that the problem wasn't my ambition or even the hard work; it was how I had been approaching success. I had pushed myself beyond my limits, believing that success required constant sacrifice. But I was wrong. There had to be a better way. That's when I began to explore the science behind achievement, human potential and what it really takes to lead a fulfilling, successful life without burnout. This exploration eventually led to the development of **The Achievement Algorithm™**.

WHY THIS BOOK IS IMPORTANT RIGHT NOW

We're in the midst of a global leadership crisis. Leaders around the world are buckling under the weight of unrelenting demands, and the cracks are beginning to show. A recent study by the World Health Organisation (2022) classified burnout as an occupational phenomenon, with over 75% of executives reporting that stress has negatively affected their mental health. These are not just statistics; they represent a real and growing problem.

The Global Leadership Forecast 2023 reveals even more alarming trends — 72% of leaders report feeling emotionally exhausted at the end of each day, a significant rise from 60% in 2020. This sharp increase in burnout is a clear indicator that the current model of leadership is unsustainable. The impact extends beyond personal health; it ripples through organisations, affecting decision-making, creativity and long-term growth.

But the cost of burnout isn't just professional, it's deeply personal. It's the missed family dinners, the holidays interrupted by work emails, the slow erosion of the passion and energy you once brought to your life outside of work. The more time you spend in this cycle, the harder it becomes to break free. Eventually, success feels more like a burden than an achievement. This is the silent trade-off that too many leaders are making and it's time for a change.

The real question isn't "How do I achieve more?" but "How do I sustain success without losing myself?". That's where this book comes in. It's not about pushing harder or sacrificing more; it's about finding a way to lead, achieve and thrive without compromising what truly matters. The Achievement Algorithm™ provides a roadmap to shift away from burnout and toward a sustainable path of success, one that supports both your professional and personal life.

THE SCIENCE BEHIND THE ACHIEVEMENT ALGORITHM

The Achievement Algorithm™ is built on cutting-edge science, integrating principles from neuroscience, behavioural psychology and quantum physics to create lasting, sustainable success. At its core, the Achievement Algorithm leverages neuroplasticity, the brain's ability to rewire itself, allowing you to shift your mindset and create new patterns that align with your goals. By understanding epigenetics, we recognise the mind-body connection — how your thoughts, beliefs and environment can actually influence gene expression, enhancing your resilience and energy. The Algorithm also teaches nervous system regulation, helping you manage stress and move from a state of "fight or flight" to calm focus, allowing for clearer decision-making and better performance.

We also harness the power of flow states, where peak performance feels effortless, and use the limbic system — the brain's emotional centre — to fuel motivation and drive. When you understand how to regulate your nervous system and tap into these states of flow, you'll find that success becomes not only achievable but sustainable. The Achievement Algorithm™ brings all of these elements together, helping you align with your true potential so that success is no longer a struggle but an empowered, fulfilling journey.

THE R.A.I.S.E FRAMEWORK: A PATH TO SUSTAINABLE LEADERSHIP

The **Achievement Algorithm™** is underpinned by our exclusive **R.A.I.S.E Framework**, which we leverage with all our clients to help them achieve sustainable success. It's designed to help leaders and high performers recognise where they are now, align their actions and mindset with their desired state and ultimately expand into new levels of success that may currently seem beyond reach.

Here's how it works:

1. **Recognise the Current State** – The first step is all about awareness. Where are you right now? What are the challenges, beliefs and patterns that are currently holding you back? Recognising the current state is essential because you can't shift what you're not aware of.
2. **Align with the Desired State** – Once you understand where you are, the next step is alignment. What's required to align your actions, mindset and habits with the state you want to achieve? This step is about closing the gap between your current reality and your desired outcome.
3. **Increase Your Capacity** – Success at a new level requires the ability to hold that level. Many people achieve brief success but can't sustain it because they haven't increased their capacity. This stage is about building the mental, emotional and physical resilience required to sustain high performance over the long term.
4. **Sustain the Desired State** – Once you've reached your desired state, the key is to sustain it. This is where many people fall short. They achieve success but quickly fall back into old habits. In this phase, we focus on embedding new habits, mindsets and systems that support long-term success.
5. **Expand Beyond Your Limits** – Finally, the most exciting part of the **R.A.I.S.E Framework** is the expansion phase. This is where you begin to push past what you previously thought was possible, opening up new realms of potential and opportunity. This is where true growth happens and where you realise that your potential is far greater than you ever imagined.

Throughout this book, you'll be guided through each phase of the **R.A.I.S.E Framework**, learning how to implement these strategies in your own life and leadership. By the end, you'll not only have the tools to achieve your current goals but also the ability to expand far beyond what you once believed was possible.

THE QUANTUM RELEASE METHOD: SHIFTING AT THE SUBCONSCIOUS LEVEL

One of the most powerful tools we use within the R.A.I.S.E Framework is our exclusive Quantum Release Method™. The Quantum Release Method™ is the fastest and most effective approach for making shifts at the subconscious level, without the need to dig into or relive past traumas or history. It's about creating lasting change at the deepest levels of your mind, so you can break free from the patterns and beliefs that have been holding you back.

Most of our behaviours, decisions and even our limits are driven by the subconscious mind, where your deepest beliefs and emotional responses are stored. Many of these beliefs were formed long ago, often based on experiences that no longer serve you, yet they continue to shape your decisions and behaviours today. This is why so many people find themselves stuck in the same patterns, even when they're consciously trying to change.

Traditional methods of personal development often involve revisiting the past, unpacking old traumas, or trying to reprogram limiting beliefs slowly over time. But the Quantum Release Method™ takes a different approach. Working directly with the subconscious mind, it allows you to release old, limiting beliefs quickly and effortlessly, creating space for new, empowering beliefs to take root. This method is not only faster but also far more effective because it works at the core level of where these beliefs are stored.

With the Quantum Release Method™, you can experience profound shifts in your mindset, confidence and behaviour in a matter of hours or days, not months or years. This makes it an invaluable tool for leaders and high achievers who want to see results quickly and maintain them over the long term.

Why Alignment Matters More Than Hustle

One of the biggest myths in the world of achievement is that the harder you work, the more you'll succeed. While hard work and discipline are important, they're not the whole story. In fact, hustle without alignment often leads to burnout, frustration and a sense of dissatisfaction, even if you're achieving your goals.

The truth is, when you're aligned — when your thoughts, beliefs and actions are working in harmony — success becomes inevitable. You don't have to force it. You don't have to grind yourself into the ground. You simply need to make the right shifts and take the right actions at the right time. That's what alignment is all about and that's exactly what you'll learn to master in this book.

WHAT THIS BOOK WILL TEACH YOU

If you're ready to go beyond traditional models of success and discover how to achieve lasting success without burnout, this book is for you. Here's what you can expect to learn:

1. **Leadership Mindset Mastery** – You'll learn how to identify and shift limiting beliefs that are holding you back and replace them with empowering beliefs that align with success.

2. **Emotional Regulation** – Discover how to manage your emotions and stress so you can stay calm, focused and in control, even in high-pressure situations.
3. **Peak Performance Strategies** – Learn how to tap into flow states, where everything feels effortless, so you can perform at your highest level without burning out.
4. **The Power of Rest and Recovery** – Understand why rest and recovery are essential for long-term success and how to incorporate them into your routine.
5. **Aligned Action** – Learn how to take action that is aligned with your goals and values so you can achieve success with more ease and momentum.
6. **Sustainable Leadership –** Learn how to lead yourself and others in a way that inspires, motivates, and empowers, while fostering long-term success and staying aligned with your core values.

THE PATH FORWARD: YOUR JOURNEY TO SUSTAINABLE SUCCESS

In summary, this book is about more than just helping you achieve your goals, it's about showing you how to do so in a way that enhances your life, fuels your passion and sustains your success over the long term. We are diving deep into the science and strategies that make sustainable leadership and personal achievement not only possible but inevitable when you're aligned with your true potential. Through the **R.A.I.S.E Framework**, you'll gain a clear understanding of how to recognise your current state, align with where you want to go, increase your capacity to hold new success, sustain it and then expand past what you once thought was possible.

The **Quantum Release Method™** will allow you to make deep subconscious shifts quickly, effectively and with lasting results. You'll learn how to release old, limiting beliefs without dragging up the past, enabling you to unlock levels of success you never imagined possible. Most importantly, this journey is about achieving success that feels good — success that doesn't drain you or compromise your health, relationships or happiness. Instead, it's about expanding into the best version of yourself, with greater ease and flow.

As you move through this book, you'll discover practical tools, actionable strategies and transformative insights that will allow you to reimagine what success can look and feel like in your life. You'll not only achieve your goals but also enjoy the process — because true success is about thriving, not just surviving.

Get ready to transform the way you think about success. This is the path to achieving more, living better and leading with purpose and passion. The journey starts here. Let's begin.

SECTION ONE

RECOGNISE — THE POWER OF CLARITY

The first step towards sustainable success is recognising where you are right now. This might seem simple but it's the foundation for all meaningful change. Without clarity, it's impossible to make the right decisions or set the right course. Recognising your current state requires an honest assessment of your challenges, beliefs and patterns. What's working for you? What's holding you back? This step is all about gaining insight into your present reality so you can clearly see the path ahead. Clarity gives you the power to shift direction and begin aligning with the life you truly want.

1

RECOGNISE — THE POWER OF CLARITY

For leaders like us, success has often been defined by external markers: revenue targets, accolades or industry recognition. But let's be honest, these aren't the true measures of success, are they? If they were, why do so many of us, after achieving these goals, still feel burnt out, dissatisfied or even a little lost? The reality is that success isn't a trophy or a finish line. It's a dynamic state of being that requires alignment with your values, intentions and capacity to sustain it over the long haul.

Success that isn't aligned with who you are at your core will never feel fulfilling. It's time to stop measuring your life by external standards and start redefining success based on what truly matters to *you*.

UNDERSTANDING WHERE YOU ARE VS. WHERE YOU WANT TO BE

Before you can achieve anything meaningful, the first step is understanding exactly where you are right now. It sounds simple, but many of us charge ahead without ever taking a real inventory of what's working and what's not. To move forward effectively, you need to define the gap between where you are and where you want to be. Think of this as your roadmap — you can't plot a course to your destination if you don't know your starting point.

Imagine standing at the foot of a mountain, looking up at the summit you want to reach. You can't simply leap to the top. You need to assess your current position, your resources and the terrain ahead before you start climbing. The same is true for leadership and success. Before you can climb, you need clarity.

THE TRADITIONAL MODEL OF SUCCESS IS FLAWED

For years, people like us have been caught in the hustle, chasing what society or industries define as "success". We've worked hard, ticked all the boxes, got the promotions, hit the targets and earned the recognition. But how often has that success felt empty? The corner office, the awards, the accolades... they look great on paper, but do they resonate with you on a deeper level?

The traditional model of "set a goal, work relentlessly, achieve and repeat" may have worked for a while, but in today's fast-paced world, this model is unsustainable. Hustle alone won't get you where you want to go, and success built on someone else's blueprint will always feel hollow. The path to real success isn't just about doing more; it's about doing what matters.

This brings us to a key point: *Are your current goals aligned with your true vision and values?* If not, it's time to reassess.

It's tempting to equate hustle with progress but let me be clear, hustle without intention is just movement without direction. Defining a goal isn't just about choosing an arbitrary target; it's about setting a trajectory that aligns with your vision and values.

The thrill of setting new goals can blur the line between what you truly want and what society expects of you. You've seen it before: the relentless chase for external markers of success that, once achieved, leave you feeling unfulfilled. That's because success is an inside job. If your ambitions aren't grounded in who you are and what you stand for, they'll never feel satisfying.

You've likely heard the saying, "Success requires sacrifice", but what's often overlooked is that *sacrifice without alignment leads to burnout*. The key is to ask yourself, *Why* are you pursuing this goal? What's driving you? Is it truly something that aligns with your core values or is it simply a reflection of external pressures? This reflection will keep your hustle intentional and meaningful.

MY JOURNEY: FROM OVERWHELM TO CLARITY

I've been exactly where you are. A few years ago, I was at the peak of my management consulting career, leading projects, travelling non-stop and constantly chasing deadlines. On the surface, I was doing everything right. I was checking off every achievement society said I should. But inside, I felt like

I was running on empty. I was overwhelmed, stressed and disconnected from everything that once mattered to me.

There came a moment when the pressure became too much. I was sitting at my desk, facing an impossible deadline and it felt like my mind just froze. No matter how hard I pushed, I couldn't think straight. The constant hustle had pushed me beyond my limits. That's when I knew something had to change.

The real turning point came when I developed the **Quantum Release Method™**. This method is the fastest and most effective way to change limiting beliefs — often instantaneously (more on this later). Unlike traditional methods that require digging into the past, the Quantum Release Method™ works directly at the subconscious level, allowing you to let go of old beliefs and adopt new ones with ease.

I combined this powerful method with nervous system rewiring audios designed specifically to solidify those belief changes at the unconscious level. This combination is what made all the difference in my life. Through this process, I rewired my brain to move from a place of overwhelm and pressure to a state of calm, focus and strategic clarity.

If you want to experience a small part of the Quantum Release Method™ for yourself, you can access the "Shift It" audio download on the Achievement Algorithm website. This will give you a taste of how quickly and effectively you can shift your emotional state and move into a place of clarity and alignment.

ALIGNING EFFORT WITH INTENTION

We've all been taught that working hard leads to success. While drive and ambition are essential, they're not enough on their own. If your efforts aren't guided by clear intention, they can feel like endless motion without meaningful progress. You might be busy, but are you really moving towards what truly matters?

The key is to align your efforts with your values and vision. The power of intention lies in its ability to focus your actions on what's genuinely important. When your intentions are clear, your mind is primed to recognise opportunities that align with your objectives. In other words, intention directs your work, ensuring that your actions are not only productive but also purposeful.

Ask yourself this: What is the deeper reason behind your current goals? How do they align with your long-term vision and values? If you're unsure about what your long-term vision and values are, now is the time to define them. If you've been in leadership or personal development for some time, this idea may not be new to you but when was the last time you really reviewed them? Life changes, and so do our goals and values, so, while this book will cover advanced elements of sustainable leadership, we're starting with the basics. Humour me; this time, we're going to do it properly. Long-term sustainable success is built on strong foundations and defining your vision and values is the bedrock of everything else that follows.

DEFINING YOUR LONG-TERM VISION: WHAT DO YOU TRULY WANT?

Your long-term vision isn't about meeting societal expectations or following a path laid out by someone else. It's about what *you* genuinely want — not what you think you *should* want, but what aligns with your deepest desires and aspirations.

If you're reading this book on sustainable leadership, it's likely that some of the things you want include more freedom, better relationships, greater health or more time for yourself and your passions. These are just examples, but your task now is to get very specific about what you want for yourself. Don't hold back or censor your desires — this is your vision and it needs to reflect what truly resonates with you.

Here's how to get started:

1. **List Five Key Things You Truly Want**
   Take a moment to think about what's most important to you. What are the five key things that, if achieved, would give you a sense of fulfilment? These could relate to different areas of your life, such as your career, relationships, health or personal growth. Let this be a moment of honesty. Write down exactly what you want, not what others expect of you.
2. **Identify How These Things Make You Feel**
   Next to each item, write how achieving it would make you feel. Would financial freedom give you peace of mind? Would improved health make you feel more energetic and empowered? It's important to connect each goal to a feeling because it helps you clarify why these goals matter and what they'll bring to your life.

3. **Script Your Vision in Detail**
   Now, take those five things and imagine that you've already achieved them. What does your life look like? Who's with you? What's your daily routine? How much time are you spending at work, with family or on your personal interests? The more detail you include, the better. Visualising this with precision gives you a clear picture of where you're heading, which will be essential as we dive deeper into the advanced strategies in this book.

This isn't just an exercise in wishful thinking — it's about gaining clarity. The clearer your vision, the easier it becomes to make decisions that align with it.

CLARIFYING YOUR VALUES: WHAT DO YOU STAND FOR?

Once you have a clear vision, it's time to define your values. These are the guiding principles that shape your decisions and actions. Without a strong sense of your core values, you may find yourself achieving goals that don't bring you the fulfilment you expected.

But here's the catch: you need to be brutally honest about what your values actually are, not what you think they *should* be. It's easy to get caught up in societal expectations, but the purpose of this exercise is to define the values that resonate with who you are right now.

1. **Identify Three Core Values**
   Start by listing three values that are most important to you. For some, these may include family, freedom or health. For others, they may be creativity, integrity or growth. Whatever they are, make sure they reflect what you genuinely care about, not what you think you ought to prioritise.
2. **Assess Whether Your Actions Align With Your Values**
   Now comes the hard part. Take a good look at whether your current actions align with these values. For example, if you value family but find that work is consistently pulling you away from spending quality time with loved ones, there's a disconnect. If you value health but neglect exercise or self-care due to your busy schedule, it's time to reflect on how your actions are supporting or undermining your values.
3. **Bridge the Gaps Between Values and Actions**
   Where is there a gap between your values and your actions? Identify those areas and consider what adjustments you need to make to align your daily life with what you truly value. For instance, if health is a priority but your lifestyle doesn't support it, you might need to schedule time for physical activity or create boundaries around work to ensure you're not sacrificing your well-being.

If you value relationships but find your career dominating your time, perhaps it's time to rethink how you structure your days or what boundaries you can set to ensure you're nurturing the connections that matter most. It's not about doing everything at once but about being intentional in how you live according to your values.

WHY VISION AND VALUES MATTER FOR SUSTAINABLE SUCCESS

You might be wondering why we're focusing so heavily on vision and values when talking about sustainable leadership. It's simple; without a clear understanding of what you're working towards and what guides your decisions, you're likely to burn out or feel unfulfilled, even if you achieve your goals.

Sustainable success isn't just about hitting short-term targets. It's about building a life that's aligned with your values and deeply satisfying over the long haul. Your vision gives you direction and your values ensure that you stay true to yourself along the way. This combination creates a foundation for lasting success, not just fleeting accomplishments.

With a clear vision and strong values, decision-making becomes easier. You'll be able to say no to opportunities or commitments that don't align with your long-term goals, which frees up your time and energy to focus on what really matters. This is the secret to not only achieving success but doing so in a way that feels deeply fulfilling and sustainable.

A REAL-WORLD EXAMPLE: VALUES-BASED LEADERSHIP IN ACTION

Consider the leadership of Richard Branson, the founder of Virgin Group. Branson's long-term vision wasn't just about building a profitable business empire, it was about creating innovative companies that challenged the status quo and put people first. His values of adventure, fun and a people-centred approach have guided Virgin's success across multiple industries.

When Virgin Atlantic was struggling in its early years, Branson refused to compromise on his values, even when it would have been easier to follow industry norms. He prioritised customer service and employee satisfaction over short-term profits, which helped differentiate Virgin from its competitors. This alignment of values with his vision of building a company people loved to work for and fly with has been a key factor in his long-term success.

Branson's story highlights that when your vision and values are aligned, you're not just working hard — you're working on something that truly matters to you and that resonates with others. This is what builds sustainable success.

BUILDING A LIFE ALIGNED WITH YOUR VISION AND VALUES

As you move forward, remember that long-term success isn't about how much you can achieve in the shortest amount of time. It's about achieving the right things in a way that aligns with your core values and brings you fulfilment. That's what makes it sustainable.

Take the time to define your vision and clarify your values. Reflect on how well your current actions align with both and make the necessary adjustments to close any gaps. It's not always easy to live in alignment with your values, especially when external pressures push you in different directions, but when you do, you'll find that success comes not only in external achievements but also in the sense of fulfilment and balance you feel within.

In the chapters ahead, we'll delve into advanced strategies for leadership and success. But everything we build on will come back to these basics: knowing what you want and staying true to your values. This is how you crack the code to sustainable success — by aligning your efforts with intention and living in a way that feels right for *you*.

CHAPTER ONE CHECKLIST FOR THE POWER OF CLARITY

1. **Reflect on Your Current Reality**
   Take an honest look at where you are right now. What's working in your life and leadership? What's holding you back? Gaining clarity on your current situation is crucial for making meaningful progress.
2. **Define the Gap Between Where You Are and Where You Want to Be**
   Understand the difference between your present state and your desired future. This awareness helps you chart a clear path toward your goals and ensures you're heading in the right direction.
3. **Clarify Your Long-Term Vision**
   Identify what you truly want for yourself, not what others expect. Define your long-term vision in detail, whether it's more freedom, better health, stronger relationships or more time for personal fulfilment.
4. **Align Your Actions With Your Core Values**
   Be honest about the values that matter most to you. Ensure that your daily actions reflect those values. If there's a disconnect, make adjustments to bring your life into alignment with what truly matters.
5. **Bridge the Gap for Sustainable Success**
   Examine where your actions are misaligned with your values and vision. Focus on bridging that gap, as long-term, sustainable success comes from living in alignment with what's important to you.

By following these steps, you can lay the foundation for a life of sustainable success — one that is both fulfilling and aligned with your true values.

2

THE SCIENCE OF CHANGE: REWIRING YOUR BRAIN FOR SUCCESS

Most people think that when things aren't going the way they want, or when progress feels impossible, there's something fundamentally wrong with them. They believe that they're broken, flawed or lacking in some essential way. But I want to offer you a different perspective. What if there wasn't anything fundamentally wrong with you? What if it wasn't a personal flaw but simply a glitch in the operating system? A small error that can be easily corrected.

Will you think differently with me for a brief moment? I'd like you to consider something, not because it's guaranteed to be 100% true, but because when I've approached things this way with people before, we've achieved remarkable results. It's like playing a board game together: we agree on the rules and share the same mindset because it allows us to play the game effectively — and to win.

Now, here's the key idea: the thing that controls how we show up and how we get things done (or don't) is largely driven by how the subconscious mind processes information. If there's a blip or glitch in an otherwise well-functioning processor, it can cause you to react in ways that don't serve you. The great news is that once you recognise this, once you see that it's just a glitch and not some permanent flaw in your wiring, it can be fixed. That shift in perspective is the first step toward unlocking the sustainable success you're aiming for.

What's fascinating about this idea is how science supports the idea that we can change not only our behaviours but also our beliefs and thought patterns. Neuroplasticity, for example, is the brain's ability to rewire itself and it's at the core of how we can transform our thinking and actions for lasting success. When you engage in practices like the **Quantum Release Method™ or nervous system rewiring audios like those within our Resilient Leader Programme**, you're literally creating new neural pathways that support your new beliefs.

I remember a day when I was faced with a high-stakes project that would have typically triggered my stress and anxiety, but this time, something was different. Instead of feeling overwhelmed, I applied the **Quantum Release Method™**. Within minutes, the usual anxiety that would have clouded my thinking was gone, replaced by a sense of calm and clarity. I made strategic decisions quickly and moved forward without feeling the heavy weight of pressure I used to carry. This wasn't a temporary fix; it was a shift in how my mind approached challenges.

That's the power of neuroplasticity: we can reprogram our brains for success. But the key to this transformation lies in understanding how the brain really works — especially the **subconscious mind**, which controls 95% of our actions and decisions. If you've ever felt like you're stuck in the same patterns no matter how hard you try to change, it's likely because your subconscious programming hasn't shifted. And contrary to popular belief, these changes can occur in moments rather than taking weeks or years. This is precisely what we tackle at The Achievement Algorithm—helping you reprogram your subconscious mind to break free from ingrained patterns and achieve lasting transformation

THE SUBCONSCIOUS: YOUR SILENT DECISION-MAKER

The subconscious mind isn't logical like your conscious mind. You can't reason with it or simply will it into change. It operates on an entirely different level, responding to **symbols, metaphors and imagery**. This is why traditional methods of change often fall short — they're trying to speak to the conscious mind when the real driver of your behaviour is deeper.

That's why the methods we use with our clients are often described as different, intriguing and sometimes, even a little strange. We're tapping into the subconscious, working with the part of your mind that responds to these **non-linear cues**. By using precise techniques like **symbolic imagery**, **guided visualisations** and the **Quantum Release Method**™, we are moulding the mind in exactly the way it needs to be for real transformation to take place.

These methods might feel unconventional, but that's precisely why they work so well. We are reprogramming your internal scripts — changing the core beliefs and patterns that control your actions. Once we shift these, **you'll begin to act and behave differently without forcing it** and your results will reflect that change.

REWIRING YOUR SUBCONSCIOUS: WHY IT MATTERS

To achieve sustainable success, it's essential to work with the subconscious mind because it's the part of you that determines how you show up in the world. Whether you're confident and decisive or consistently self-doubting, those traits are all driven by deep, subconscious beliefs. **Willpower alone won't cut it**. You've probably experienced times when you've tried to push through with sheer determination, only to find yourself slipping back into old habits. That's because the subconscious is still running the show behind the scenes.

Think of the subconscious as an autopilot system. It controls the vast majority of your actions, decisions and reactions without you even realising it. This is why, if you're serious about long-term success, it's crucial to rewire your subconscious beliefs so they align with the person you want to become.

At **The Achievement Algorithm**, we work strategically with the subconscious, using methods designed to create **lasting shifts** and we can now effectively release limiting beliefs and replace them with empowering ones in a matter of minutes.

THE POWER OF SYMBOLS AND IMAGERY IN REWIRING THE BRAIN

Let's dive deeper into why symbols and imagery are so effective in rewiring the brain. When we talk about the subconscious mind, we're talking about a part of the brain that doesn't operate in a linear, logical way. It communicates through emotions, pictures and sensations. That's why the most powerful shifts happen when we use **symbolic language** to communicate with it.

For example, when you engage in a **visualisation exercise** where you picture yourself achieving a certain goal, your subconscious doesn't know the difference between imagination and reality. It accepts what you're picturing as truth and it begins to shift your internal programming to align with that new vision. Over time, as you repeat these visualisations, you're creating new neural pathways in the brain that make it easier to act in ways that support your goals.

This is also why **metaphors and symbolic exercises** are so effective. They bypass the conscious mind's defences and speak directly to the subconscious. When you use symbols that represent strength, confidence or success, your brain starts to associate those qualities with your self-image, and your behaviour shifts accordingly.

At **The Achievement Algorithm**, we've developed methods that harness this power, creating **targeted exercises** designed to rewire the subconscious in ways that lead to greater success. These techniques aren't just about thinking positively — they're about creating real, measurable changes in how your brain processes information and guides your actions.

HOW THE QUANTUM RELEASE METHOD™ REWIRES YOUR BRAIN

One of the core techniques we use is the **Quantum Release Method™**, which has the ability to create instant shifts in deeply ingrained beliefs. This method doesn't require you to dig through your past or relive old experiences. Instead, it works directly at the subconscious level, releasing limiting beliefs and replacing them with more empowering ones in a matter of minutes.

I've seen this method transform clients who've struggled with the same patterns for years. Whether it's a fear of failure, imposter syndrome or anxiety around decision-making, the **Quantum Release Method™** quickly dissolves those blocks, allowing people to move forward with clarity and confidence.

What's unique about this method is that it bypasses the need for conscious effort. You don't have to struggle to convince yourself to think differently — it happens automatically as your brain rewires itself. The old pathways that kept you stuck are replaced with new ones that support your goals and aspirations.

When combined with our **nervous system rewiring audios**, the effects of the **Quantum Release Method™** are reinforced, ensuring that the changes are not just temporary but lasting. These meditations help you embed the new beliefs deeply into your subconscious, making it easier to act in alignment with your new mindset.

USING THESE TECHNIQUES FOR SUSTAINABLE SUCCESS

What makes this approach so powerful is that it addresses the real root of change — your subconscious mind. Instead of focusing on surface-level strategies, we're going straight to the source, reprogramming the part of your brain that drives 95% of your actions.

This isn't about quick fixes or temporary motivation. It's about creating deep, lasting changes that lead to **sustainable success**. As you begin to align your subconscious with your conscious goals, you'll notice that things start to shift in ways that feel natural and effortless. You'll no longer have to fight against yourself to stay motivated or overcome challenges because your brain will be wired to support you.

The techniques we use at **The Achievement Algorithm** might seem a little unconventional but that's because they're designed to work with the subconscious in the way it actually operates. **Symbols, imagery and metaphors** are the language of the subconscious, and by using these tools, we're able to create real, lasting transformations.

In the coming chapters, we'll explore more advanced strategies for rewiring your brain and aligning your actions with your long-term vision, but remember, this journey starts by reshaping the patterns that drive your behaviour at the deepest level. Once you begin to **work with your subconscious mind** instead of against it, that's when the real breakthroughs happen. That's how you crack the code to sustainable success.

CHAPTER TWO CHECKLIST FOR THE SCIENCE OF CHANGE

Recognise the Power of Neuroplasticity

- Understand that your brain has the ability to rewire itself (neuroplasticity), allowing you to create new beliefs and behaviours for success.

Assess Your Current Beliefs

- Identify two key limiting beliefs that are holding you back. These could be beliefs like "I'm not good enough" or "I don't deserve success."
- Access the free SHIFT IT nervous system rewiring tool to begin shifting those limiting beliefs at the subconscious level. Select the two negative emotions you want to work on and follow the process.

By following this checklist, you're already on your way to rewiring your brain and setting yourself up for long-term success.

SECTION TWO

ALIGN — ALIGN WITH THE DESIRED STATE

Once you've gained clarity about where you are, the next step is to align with where you want to go. This means closing the gap between your current reality and your desired outcome. To align with the state you want to achieve, you must ensure that your actions, mindset and habits are in harmony with your goals. Alignment isn't about forcing or pushing; it's about bringing yourself into a state of flow where your daily actions support your vision for success. This is where your inner world begins to reflect in your outer results. When you're in alignment, progress feels natural, like moving with the current rather than against it. Your daily actions start to reflect your vision, and success becomes inevitable.

3

ALIGN — ALIGN WITH THE DESIRED STATE

THE POWER OF INTENTION: SETTING THE COURSE FOR SUCCESS

Intention is the starting point of any achievement. It's more than just a wish or a hope — it's a focused declaration of where you are headed. When you set an intention, you give your brain a directive, focusing its energy in a specific direction. But setting an intention alone isn't enough; your actions must align with it.

Consider the story of Jim Carrey. In 1990, as a relatively unknown comedian, he wrote himself a cheque for $10 million for "acting services rendered" and dated it five years into the future. He carried that cheque in his wallet as a daily reminder of the success he intended to achieve. By 1995, Carrey had earned that exact amount for his role in *Dumb and Dumber*. His intention wasn't just a vague wish, it was a focused effort. Every day, his actions, mindset and decisions aligned with that goal until it became a reality.

This shows us that intention isn't just about hoping for an outcome. It's about directing your mental, emotional and physical energy towards making that outcome a reality. When your intentions are clear, your mind primes itself to notice opportunities that align with your goal. Your brain becomes wired to filter out distractions, focusing on what will help you achieve success.

HOW INTENTION DRIVES SUCCESS

Setting intentions doesn't just change what you notice; it changes who you *become* in the process. This is one of the most profound aspects of intention-setting that often gets overlooked. When you decide to focus on a goal, it's not just about identifying what you want – it's about aligning yourself with that outcome, both consciously and subconsciously.

The Reticular Activating System (RAS), a network of neurons in your brainstem, plays a crucial role in this. The RAS is like the brain's filtering system, deciding what information gets through to your conscious mind and what gets left out. Think about the sheer volume of stimuli you encounter every day – sounds, sights, conversations, messages and so on. The RAS helps you focus on what's relevant based on what you've decided to prioritise.

When you set a clear intention, you effectively *programme* your RAS to filter in the people, opportunities and solutions that are aligned with your goal. It's like when you decide you want a specific type of car – suddenly, you see that car everywhere. It's not that the car wasn't there before but your brain wasn't filtering it in as important. The same thing happens with your intentions. When you focus on a goal, your brain starts noticing everything connected to that goal.

But here's where it gets even more powerful. Setting intentions is not just about noticing things that align with your desires — it's about transformation. It fundamentally changes how you think and how you act. Every new goal or intention requires you to *evolve* into a new version of yourself to achieve it.

THE TRANSFORMATIVE POWER OF INTENTION

When you set an intention, you're not just stating a desire; you're initiating a process of personal evolution. Each intention you set asks something of you. It demands that you grow, adapt and stretch beyond your current limits. It's not just about putting in more hours or working harder; it's about stepping into a version of yourself that can make that intention a reality.

For example, if you set an intention to grow your business, you're not just intending for more clients, higher revenue or bigger opportunities. You're also intending to become the type of leader who can handle those things. You might need to develop greater confidence, improve your delegation skills or sharpen your strategic thinking. Setting the intention means you begin to notice the habits, thoughts and actions that no longer serve you and that awareness propels you to make changes.

A powerful question to ask yourself when setting intentions is: *Who do I need to become to make this happen?* The answer will often highlight areas for growth, whether that's developing resilience, stepping into leadership with more authority or letting go of fears that have been holding you back.

INTENTION UNLOCKS POTENTIAL YOU DIDN'T KNOW YOU HAD

What's fascinating about this process is that it often reveals potential within you that you weren't fully aware of. By focusing your mind on a specific intention, you start to unlock resources, skills and strengths you might not have consciously tapped into before.

Let's take an example of someone setting an intention to be more present and engaged in their personal life, especially with family. At first, it might feel challenging – habits of being distracted or prioritising work may be ingrained. But as that intention solidifies, they start to notice opportunities to connect with their loved ones in new ways. It might be small at first – an extra five minutes at the dinner table or a focused conversation with their partner – but these small shifts compound and, over time, they transform not only how that person interacts with their family but also how they perceive their own identity as a family member.

THE SHIFT FROM DOING TO BECOMING

The magic of intention is that it shifts your focus from *doing* more to *becoming* more. Many people approach their goals from a place of action alone – "What do I need to *do* to achieve this?", but intention teaches us that success doesn't come from just doing more. It comes from *becoming* the kind of person who naturally creates the outcomes you desire.

Imagine setting an intention to be a more decisive leader. The intention isn't just about making faster decisions; it's about becoming the kind of leader who feels confident, clear and unshaken in their decision-making process. With that intention, you start to notice the patterns of hesitation that have held you back in the past. You become aware of the moments when you could take charge and step forward with more clarity.

This isn't about forcing change. It's about aligning with the version of yourself that already exists within you, the one that is capable of achieving your intention.

THE BRAIN'S RESPONSE TO INTENTION

Scientific research supports this transformative process. Studies on neuroplasticity, the brain's ability to rewire itself, show that when we set intentions and repeatedly focus on them, we create new neural pathways. These pathways make it easier for us to think, act and behave in ways that are aligned with our goals.

For example, when you set an intention to become more confident in public speaking, you are training your brain to think and respond differently in those situations. As you practice and visualise success, your brain starts to build new connections that make it easier to access that confidence the next time you step on stage. Over time, the brain strengthens these pathways and what once felt difficult becomes second nature. This is how intention leads to transformation — by rewiring the brain to support your desired state.

THE SUBTLE SHIFT IN PERCEPTION

What makes intention so powerful is the subtle shift in perception it creates. Once you've set a clear intention, you're no longer looking at the world through the lens of "I wish this could happen" but instead through the lens of "I am becoming the person who can make this happen". This shift changes how you interpret everything, from challenges and obstacles to opportunities and possibilities.

In the past, you may have seen a setback as a sign that you're not cut out for success but when you're aligned with a clear intention, those same setbacks become learning experiences, stepping stones toward your goal. You start to see everything as working in your favour because your mind is now filtering the world through the lens of your intention.

This is why setting intentions is so much more than just hoping for success. It's about creating a powerful shift in how you show up in the world — how you think, how you act and who you become in the process. When your intention is clear and your actions align with it success isn't just possible, it's inevitable.

WHAT DOES YOUR GOAL REQUIRE FROM YOU?

Once your intention is set, the next crucial step is understanding what your goal actually *demands* from you. This is where many people fall short. They set big, bold goals but continue to operate with the same mindset, habits and actions that have kept them stuck in their current reality. The truth is that achieving new results requires you to *become* a new version of yourself.

Think about it: if your goal is to grow your business or advance in your career, you have to ask yourself some tough but important questions. *What kind of leader do I need to be to make this happen?* Does this goal require you to become more strategic? Do you need to be more resilient in the face of setbacks or more comfortable with taking risks? Perhaps the goal demands that you develop better delegation skills or become more adaptable when things don't go according to plan.

This is where people often get stuck. They believe that success is just about doing more of what they've always done. But doing more of the same will only get you more of the same. To achieve your goal, you need to *become* more. Success demands that you evolve into the kind of person who can not only reach your goal but thrive in the environment that comes with it. The challenges, responsibilities and rewards that come with any significant goal will be different from what you're used to and the only way to handle them is to grow into the person who is ready for them.

THE EVOLUTION REQUIRED FOR SUCCESS

Let's break it down. Every goal you set is asking something of you. Whether it's more focus, more discipline, more courage, or more adaptability, your goal is calling you to become the person who embodies these traits.

For instance, if your goal is to double your business revenue, you're not just asking yourself to work harder or put in more hours, you're asking yourself to think at a higher level. You might need to shift from a hands-on, task-oriented approach to a more visionary, big-picture strategy. You'll need to become someone who can see opportunities for growth, navigate risks and make decisions quickly, without getting bogged down by the details. Perhaps you need to cultivate more trust in your team, delegating responsibilities and empowering others to take the lead in areas where you don't need to be involved.

Let's say your goal is personal — perhaps improving your health or creating more balance in your life. This might require you to let go of habits that no longer serve you, like burning the candle at both ends or neglecting your physical well-being. To align with this goal, you may need to become someone who prioritises self-care, says "no" to distractions and develops boundaries to protect your time and energy.

THE POWER OF IDENTITY SHIFTS

This concept is often referred to as an *identity shift*. To achieve something you've never done before, you have to step into the identity of someone who has already achieved it. Think of it this way: every goal you set creates a gap between your current self and your future self. The key to closing that gap isn't just about working harder or faster; it's about evolving into the person who lives that reality.

You can't achieve new outcomes while operating with the same mindset and behaviours that brought you to your current state. That's why you need to align every part of your life with the vision of your goal. It's not just about setting intentions; it's about *becoming* the person who naturally achieves those results.

PRACTICAL STEPS TO BECOMING MORE

To really drive this point home, consider these practical steps in shifting your identity to align with your goals:

1. **Map Out the Characteristics of Your Future Self**: Start by visualising the version of yourself who has already achieved your goal. What qualities do they have? What kind of mindset do they operate from? How do they handle challenges, decisions, and opportunities? Get specific. Whether it's more patience, decisiveness or resilience, identify exactly what you need to cultivate within yourself.
2. **Change Your Internal Dialogue**: How you talk to yourself is critical. The person you are now might face challenges with hesitation or self-doubt. The person who has already achieved your goal approaches the same challenges with confidence and clarity. Begin to adopt the language and mindset of your future self. Start speaking as though you *are* that person, even if it feels uncomfortable at first.
3. **Upgrade Your Habits**: Success is the result of consistent action. What daily habits does your future self engage in that you are not currently prioritising? Whether it's exercising regularly, setting aside time for creative thinking or blocking out distractions, focus on building habits that align with the person you are becoming.
4. **Expand Your Comfort Zone**: Growth only happens when you stretch beyond what feels familiar. If your goal demands that you become more resilient, you'll need to start facing discomfort head-on, whether that means taking risks, having difficult conversations or stepping into leadership roles you might have previously avoided. Every time you push past your current limits, you're training yourself to operate at a higher level.

5. **Cultivate Emotional Resilience**: Every goal, no matter how exciting, will come with challenges and setbacks. What separates successful people from the rest is their ability to handle these moments without losing sight of their vision. Building emotional resilience — learning how to stay calm, focused and adaptable when things don't go as planned — is a crucial part of becoming the person your goal requires you to be.

WHO DO YOU NEED TO BECOME?

A powerful way to keep yourself aligned with your goals is to continuously ask: *Who do I need to become to achieve this?* This question shifts your focus from external factors (like workload, obstacles or even timing) to internal growth. It reframes the challenge, encouraging you to step up and evolve into a new version of yourself.

When you approach your goals from this mindset, you're no longer just ticking tasks off a list — you're engaging in deep personal transformation. And that's the key to not only achieving success but sustaining it.

If you want to grow your business, take on a leadership role or even just become more balanced in your personal life, remember that the external success you're striving for is a reflection of the internal growth you commit to. The more you evolve, the more aligned you'll become with the outcomes you desire.

USING PERSONAS FOR SUCCESS: A REAL-LIFE EXAMPLE

Stepping into a new persona allows you to bypass limiting beliefs and access qualities that serve your success. Beyoncé's Sasha Fierce wasn't about pretending — it was a way to harness confidence and overcome fear. Another example is David Bowie, who used personas like Ziggy Stardust to push the boundaries of his creativity. These personas helped both artists unlock parts of themselves that were necessary for their success.

When you adopt a persona, you're not faking it — you're embodying the qualities of the person you need to be to achieve your goals. You're aligning with a future version of yourself who has already accomplished what you're striving for.

TWO POWERFUL TOOLS FOR GOAL ALIGNMENT

Let's talk about two practical tools that help you align with your desired state:

1. **Taking on a New Persona** To align with your goals, create a persona that represents the person who has already achieved them. Get clear on how this person behaves, thinks and handles challenges. Give this persona a name and when things get tough, step into that identity. This tool helps you tap into the mindset and qualities you need to cultivate to succeed.
2. **The Pyramid of Identity** This exercise helps you visualise where you are versus where you need to be. Imagine two pyramids: the first represents your current self and the second represents the person who has achieved your goal. Break down each pyramid into layers — environment, actions, habits, beliefs and identity. Identify where the gaps are and focus on aligning these layers with the person who has already achieved your goal.

These tools guide you in embodying the traits, beliefs, and actions that lead to sustainable success. By adopting the mindset of someone who has already succeeded, you naturally start to behave in ways that align with your goals.

ALIGNING YOUR GOALS WITH YOUR LONG-TERM VISION

It's easy to get caught up in short-term wins or external markers of success, but true fulfilment comes from aligning your goals with your long-term vision. Your vision is the bigger picture of the life you want, encompassing your career, relationships, health and personal growth. When your goals are in harmony with this vision, every step you take moves you closer to creating a life that feels deeply meaningful.

CHAPTER THREE CHECKLIST FOR ALIGNING WITH YOUR DESIRED STATE

Here's a simple checklist to help you align with your desired state:

- **Set a Clear Intention:** What do you want to achieve, and why does it matter to you?
- **Ask What Your Goal Requires:** What shifts in your mindset, habits or behaviours do you need to make to achieve this goal?
- **Use the Pyramid of Identity:** Identify where you are now and where you need to be to achieve your goal. Align your beliefs, habits and actions with the identity of someone who has already succeeded.
- **Adopt a New Persona:** Step into the mindset and behaviours of the version of yourself who has already achieved your goal.
- **Align Your Goals With Your Long-Term Vision:** Make sure your goals aren't just about short-term wins but are moving you toward a more fulfilling life.

By following these steps, you'll not only set clear goals but also align your actions and mindset with the success you desire. The journey becomes less about pushing and more about flowing naturally toward your vision. This is how you align with sustainable success.

4

ANCHORING IN THE NEW VISION

Visualisation is one of the most powerful tools at your disposal. It's a practice that allows you to mentally rehearse success and prepare both your brain and body for the outcomes you desire. It's not just a motivational trick; it's a proven method that world-class athletes, leaders and innovators use to elevate their performance and overcome obstacles.

At its core, visualisation involves vividly imagining your goals and desired outcomes. When done right, it not only boosts your confidence but primes your brain for success. This technique is a game-changer for leaders like us, who are striving to break free from limiting beliefs and create sustainable success.

WHY VISUALISATION WORKS: THE SCIENCE BEHIND IT

Here's the science bit: when you vividly imagine yourself achieving a goal, your brain activates many of the same neural pathways that would fire if you were actually doing it. In other words, your brain doesn't fully distinguish between a real experience and an imagined one. This is why visualisation can be such a powerful practice — it allows you to mentally prepare for success before you even take action.

Research shows that this kind of mental rehearsal improves performance, strengthens focus and builds confidence. Neuroscience has proven that our brains are capable of change through a concept known as neuroplasticity, which means we can train our minds to develop new patterns and break free from limiting beliefs.

Visualisation and mental rehearsal are not just feel-good practices, they're scientifically backed techniques with a growing body of research to support their effectiveness in achieving personal and professional goals. One of the most famous studies demonstrating the power of visualisation was conducted by Dr. Biasiotto at the University of Chicago. It focused on improving basketball free-throw performance.

THE BASKETBALL STUDY

In this experiment, Dr. Biasiotto divided participants into three groups. The first group practised shooting free throws every day for thirty days. The second group didn't practice at all but instead, visualised themselves successfully making free throws each day. The third group did neither. The results were astonishing. The group that physically practised improved their free-throw performance by 24%. However, the group that only visualised themselves making free throws improved by 23% — nearly the same as the group that practised daily!

This study shows that mental rehearsal through visualisation can have nearly the same impact as physical practice because, during visualisation, your brain fires the same neurons as it would if you were actually doing the activity. The brain begins to treat the imagined scenario as real, reinforcing the neural pathways necessary to succeed.

NEUROPLASTICITY AND THE BRAIN'S ABILITY TO CHANGE

Neuroplasticity, the brain's ability to rewire itself, is at the heart of why visualisation and subconscious programming work so well. Dr. Michael Merzenich, a leading neuroscientist and pioneer in the field of brain plasticity, conducted groundbreaking studies proving that the adult brain can change and adapt its structure based on new learning and experiences.

One experiment in particular demonstrated the power of neuroplasticity. In a study involving stroke patients who had lost movement in one of their hands, Dr. Merzenich and his team showed that intensive physical therapy combined with mental visualisation helped patients regain mobility. The patients were asked to repeatedly imagine their hands moving and completing tasks and, over time, the brain began to reorganise itself. This combination of physical and mental practice allowed new neural connections to form, ultimately restoring functionality.

The implications of this study are huge for personal development. If visualisation can help stroke patients recover lost motor skills, it can certainly help you rewire your brain to overcome limiting beliefs and adopt new, success-oriented behaviours. Here are a few science-backed examples supporting the science of visualisation.

THE POWER OF MENTAL IMAGERY IN ATHLETES

A meta-analysis of sports psychology studies, conducted by researcher Patrick G. Weinberg and his colleagues, found that visualisation and mental imagery improve athletic performance across a wide range of sports. Athletes who used mental imagery techniques, such as visualising themselves successfully performing specific movements or winning competitions, consistently outperformed those who didn't.

This research supports the notion that mental rehearsal can improve not only physical performance but also mental and emotional readiness. By repeatedly visualising success, athletes create neural pathways that enhance their ability to perform under pressure — just like you can when you visualise success in business, leadership or personal growth.

THE SUBCONSCIOUS MIND AND SYMBOLS: THE WORK OF DR. CARL JUNG

Swiss psychiatrist, Carl Jung, one of the founders of analytical psychology, spent much of his career studying the subconscious mind and the role of symbols, imagery and archetypes. Jung's research demonstrated that the subconscious communicates in a different language than the conscious mind, responding more deeply to metaphors and symbolic representations.

Jung's work in dream analysis showed that symbols hold deep, personal and collective meanings that can shape our beliefs and behaviours. For example, a symbol of strength or success that resonates with you can have a powerful influence on your subconscious mind, guiding your decisions and actions in alignment with your goals. This is why visualisation, guided imagery and metaphorical exercises are such effective tools for change.

In a practical sense, when you repeatedly expose your subconscious to positive imagery — whether it's seeing yourself confidently delivering a presentation or visualising a successful business negotiation — you are communicating with the subconscious in its own language. You are telling your brain that this is who you are and what you're capable of, leading to real-world changes in behaviour and results.

PROGRAMMING THE SUBCONSCIOUS: THE WORK OF DR. BRUCE LIPTON

Dr. Bruce Lipton, a stem cell biologist and pioneer in the field of epigenetics, has extensively researched how the subconscious mind affects our lives. In his book, *The Biology of Belief*, Lipton explains how our beliefs, especially subconscious ones, shape our reality. He argues that most of our behaviours, habits and even our health are controlled by subconscious programming that we've developed throughout our lives.

Lipton's work shows that by changing these subconscious beliefs through methods like visualisation, affirmations and imagery, we can change our biology, enhance our health and achieve our goals more effectively. He likens the subconscious to a hard drive running programs in the background. If you want to change your reality, you must rewrite the programmes stored in the subconscious mind. And the best way to rewrite those programs is by engaging the mind in visualisations and metaphors that speak its language.

At *The Achievement Algorithm,* we tap into these scientific findings by focusing on methods that work directly with the subconscious mind. Through tools like the *Quantum Release Method*™ and our visualisation techniques, we help rewire those limiting beliefs and turn them into empowering ones. This isn't just theory; it's rooted in neuroscience and psychology.

VISUALISATION IN ACTION: REAL-LIFE SUCCESS STORIES

To truly understand the power of visualisation, let's look at a couple of examples from people who have mastered this technique and used it to reach incredible heights.

Take Muhammad Ali, for example, one of the greatest boxers of all time. Ali didn't just train his body for the ring; he trained his mind too. Before each fight, Ali would visualise every aspect of the match, from stepping into the ring to throwing the winning punch. He didn't just see the victory in his mind; he felt it. He lived the experience before it even happened. This wasn't just positive thinking; it was a mental workout. By consistently practising visualisation, Ali conditioned both his mind and body for success, allowing him to enter each fight with the confidence of someone who had already won.

Another shining example is Jack Nicklaus, one of the greatest golfers in history. Nicklaus would mentally rehearse each shot before he even stepped up to the tee. He would visualise the trajectory of the ball, where it would land and the mechanics of his swing. This wasn't a one-off exercise; it was part of his routine. By the time he was physically taking the shot, his mind and body had already been through the process. This method of mental rehearsal helped him perform under pressure and achieve consistent success throughout his career.

Now, you may not be stepping into a boxing ring or onto a golf course, but leaders like us face our own high-pressure moments and big goals. Whether you're leading a team through a challenging project, aiming for a promotion or scaling a business, visualisation is a tool that can help you break through your barriers.

BRINGING VISUALISATION INTO YOUR LEADERSHIP PRACTICE

So, how can you start using visualisation to break through your limiting beliefs and achieve your long-term vision? It's not about spending hours in deep meditation; just a few focused minutes a day can make all the difference.

1. **Mental Contrasting**
   While visualising success is key, it's equally important to be realistic about the challenges you might face. Mental contrasting involves picturing both the positive outcomes and potential obstacles. By preparing yourself for setbacks, you not only stay optimistic but also build resilience. You're ready for whatever comes your way.
2. **Guided Imagery**
   Think of guided imagery as your mental dress rehearsal. Let's say you're preparing for a crucial presentation or business pitch. Don't just hope for the best, mentally rehearse it. Picture yourself walking into the room with confidence, delivering your key points with clarity and getting the positive response you want. Visualise every detail: the expressions on people's faces, the sound of applause. By the time you walk into that

room for real, you'll feel like you've already done it, which can significantly reduce any nerves or anxiety.

3. **Sensory Visualisation**
   Success is more than just achieving a goal — it's an experience. Sensory visualisation involves engaging all five senses as you picture your success. What does it look like? What can you hear? How does it feel? For example, if you're leading a major project, picture yourself standing in the office when it's completed. Hear the congratulations, feel the sense of accomplishment and even imagine the physical surroundings. The more vividly you can imagine it, the more real it becomes to your brain.
4. **Future Self Visualisation**
   One of the most powerful forms of visualisation is stepping into your future self. Picture the version of you who has already achieved your long-term goals. How does this future self act? What decisions do they make? What are their habits? By imagining yourself as the person you want to become, you start to adopt the thoughts, behaviours and actions that will get you there. This isn't just a daydream; it's a mental framework that shapes your present actions to align with your future success.
5. **Progressive Visualisation**
   Big goals can sometimes feel overwhelming, especially if you're still wrestling with limiting beliefs. Progressive visualisation helps to break those big dreams into smaller, actionable steps. Instead of just focusing on the end result, mentally rehearse each stage of the process. Celebrate the small wins along the way to stay motivated and focused. It's about enjoying the journey as much as the destination.

Imagine viewing your future laid out in front of you on a timeline from a bird's-eye perspective. Visualise yourself 12, 6, and 3 months into the future. Now ask yourself: What steps did I take, and what events unfolded to get me there? By asking powerful questions, we unlock powerful answers. The subconscious mind is a natural problem-solving machine, and if you dedicate time to this technique, you might be surprised by the insights that come to you.

THE LINK BETWEEN VISUALISATION AND THE QUANTUM RELEASE METHOD™

The Quantum Release Method™ is the fastest way to shift limiting beliefs, but visualisation is the key to reinforcing that change. Once you've identified and released those mental blocks, you need a tool to help keep you on track. This is where visualisation comes in. It strengthens the new, empowering beliefs you've created and helps you stay aligned with your long-term vision.

Think of it like building a house. The Quantum Release Method™ lays the foundation by removing the old, crumbling structures of limiting beliefs. Visualisation is the blueprint and the construction process that allows you to build something new. Together, these methods create a powerful combination for breaking through barriers and achieving sustainable success.

KEY TAKEAWAYS: VISUALISATION AND SUSTAINABLE SUCCESS

1. **Visualisation is a mental rehearsal for success.** It primes your brain and body to perform at their best by mentally practising the actions you need to take to achieve your goals.
2. **Top performers swear by it.** Leaders, athletes and innovators use visualisation to overcome obstacles and reach the top of their game. It's not just for sports stars, it's for people like us, too.
3. **It rewires your brain.** Visualisation helps to create new neural pathways, breaking down old patterns of limiting beliefs and reinforcing a mindset of success.
4. **Start small but start now.** Even five minutes of guided visualisation each day can make a huge difference in how you approach your goals. It's about building the habit.
5. **Combine it with the Quantum Release Method™.** Visualisation reinforces the breakthroughs you achieve through the Quantum Release Method™, giving you the tools to keep moving forward towards your vision.

CHAPTER FOUR CHECKLIST: HOW TO USE VISUALISATION TO BREAK THROUGH BARRIERS

To help you get started with visualisation, here's a step-by-step guide:

Identify Your Goal

- What specific outcome do you want to achieve?
- What limiting beliefs are standing in your way?

Set Aside Time for Visualisation

- Dedicate at least five minutes each day to practise visualisation.
- Make it a consistent part of your routine, whether in the morning, before important meetings or at the end of the day.

Use Guided Imagery

- Picture yourself achieving your goal in vivid detail.
- Engage all your senses — what do you see, hear and feel when you've achieved it?

Prepare for Obstacles

- Practise mental contrasting. Visualise both the successful outcome and the challenges you might face.
- Mentally rehearse how you will overcome any setbacks that may arise.

Step Into Your Future Self

- Visualise yourself as the person who has already achieved the success you desire.
- Ask yourself: how does my future self think, act, and behave?

Pair It With the Quantum Release Method™

- Use visualisation to reinforce the breakthroughs you achieve through the Quantum Release Method™.
- Visualise yourself living free from limiting beliefs, fully embracing your potential.

By incorporating visualisation into your routine, you're not just imagining success, you're preparing your brain and body to make it a reality. Combined with the power of the Quantum Release Method™, this practice can help you break through limiting beliefs, align with your long-term vision and achieve sustainable success without sacrificing happiness along the way.

5

BREAKING THROUGH LIMITING BELIEFS FOR SUSTAINABLE SUCCESS

We touched upon limiting beliefs briefly in Chapter One, but this topic warrants its own focused chapter. Why? Because our beliefs lay the foundation for every inch of our sustainable success.

Imagine running a marathon with an invisible weight. You're well-prepared and fully capable of reaching the finish line, yet this unseen weight drags you down, making every step feel heavier than it should. For leaders like us — ambitious people striving for success — this invisible weight represents our **limiting beliefs**. They quietly hold us back, making sustainable success seem harder to achieve than it really is.

Our ultimate goal is to create **sustainable success** — the kind of long-term growth that doesn't just look good on paper but aligns with who we are and the life we want to live. But to get there, we need to understand the invisible barriers in our minds that keep us from reaching our full potential. These limiting beliefs, those nagging doubts about whether we deserve to succeed or whether happiness and success can truly coexist, are like weights that slow our progress.

THE SUBTLE SABOTAGE OF LIMITING BELIEFS

Beliefs are the silent architects behind every decision we make. Limiting beliefs, however, are those sneaky, internalised messages that act as barriers to growth. They manifest in various ways: as excuses, fears or justifications for why something can't be done. They can be subtle, masquerading as rational thinking or self-preservation, but the truth is, they hold us back from taking the risks that could propel us forward. It's like driving a car with the handbrake on – you may still move but you'll never reach full speed.

Take Howard Schultz, for example, the former CEO of Starbucks. He didn't just see Starbucks as a coffee shop; he believed it could be a "third place" for people to gather, somewhere between home and work. That empowering belief shaped his decisions and led Starbucks to global success. If Schultz had been constrained by the limiting belief that Starbucks was just another coffee shop, the brand's potential might never have been realised.

On the other hand, limiting beliefs can quietly sabotage even the most experienced leaders. For instance, a business founder might believe, "My company can't survive a downturn," and as a result, they may avoid innovation or make overly conservative decisions out of fear. The irony? This defensive stance often leads to stagnation, making the limiting belief a self-fulfilling prophecy.

We all have limiting beliefs, especially around success and happiness. Maybe you've caught yourself thinking, "If I'm successful, I'll lose my personal life," or, "Success comes with stress, and I just want to be happy." These beliefs feel protective, but they're actually the invisible weight holding you back from claiming the sustainable success you deserve.

HOW LIMITING BELIEFS BLOCK BOTH SUCCESS AND HAPPINESS

Limiting beliefs don't just stop us from achieving success, they also block us from experiencing happiness once we've reached our goals. Let's be honest, how often have you hit a milestone only to feel an unexpected sense of dissatisfaction, as if something was missing? You thought that hitting your target would bring a sense of fulfilment but instead, there's a lingering emptiness. That's because, deep down, many of us believe that success and happiness can't coexist. Or worse, that we aren't truly deserving of both.

These beliefs are subtle, operating quietly in the background, convincing us that success demands sacrifice. It's like a mental contract we've signed without realising it, thinking, "If I achieve this level of success, I'll have to give up something else — my health, my relationships or my peace of mind", and so, even as we move closer to our goals, we hold back from fully embracing the opportunities in front of us. We sabotage our own happiness because, deep down, we're afraid of the consequences of having it all.

For many of us, the most powerful limiting belief is that **success comes with a price**. It's a price we think we have to pay in time, health, or relationships. This belief drives us to make decisions that ultimately limit our growth. We may not take risks, we may shy away from certain opportunities, or we may hesitate to fully celebrate our wins, all because we're afraid of what we might lose in exchange for our success.

Here's where things get interesting: **sustainable success** doesn't require us to sacrifice happiness. In fact, true, long-lasting success depends on finding harmony between the two. Sustainable success isn't about constantly pushing harder and harder while neglecting your own well-being; it's about aligning your goals with the things that genuinely bring you joy and fulfilment. It's about living a life where success fuels your happiness rather than depleting it.

THE NATURE OF LIMITING BELIEFS

We all have limiting beliefs — those mental barriers that hold us back from pursuing bigger goals or even from achieving the objectives we set for ourselves in our daily lives. These beliefs often form as a way for the mind to protect us from perceived risks, challenges or potential failure. At first, they might seem like a shield, keeping us "safe", but in reality, they restrict our growth and potential, creating invisible boundaries that prevent us from thriving.

Think about it like this: your mind is trying to keep you in a comfort zone. Every time you start to stretch beyond that, the mental barriers kick in. "Is it really worth the risk?", "What if you fail?", "Can you handle success?". These questions seem protective but are actually part of the defence mechanism that holds you back.

The National Science Foundation estimates that we generate up to 50,000 thoughts each day, and here's the kicker: 95% of those thoughts are the same ones we had the day before. The same loops, the same doubts and the same self-imposed limitations. This repetition shapes not only how we view the world but also how we act in it. Over time, these repeated thoughts harden into beliefs — beliefs that shape our mindset. And that mindset, whether positive or limiting, drives the actions we take. Those actions, in turn, determine the results we see in our lives.

THE POWER OF BELIEFS

As we move through life, the beliefs we hold dictate the choices we make, the risks we take and the limits we place on ourselves. Psychologist Robert M. emphasises this in his research, explaining how deeply our beliefs impact not just our decisions, but our very sense of self.

He says:

> *"Beliefs are like filters on a camera. What the camera 'sees' is a function of the filters through which it is viewing its subject. In other words, how we 'see' the world is a function of our beliefs and profoundly influences personality. As a result of our beliefs, we define ourselves as worthy or worthless, powerful or powerless, competent or incompetent, trusting or suspicious, belonging or outcast, self-reliant or dependent, flexible or judgmental, fairly treated or victimised, loved or hated. Your beliefs have far-reaching consequences, both positive and negative, in your life. Beliefs affect your moods, relationships, job performance, self-esteem, physical health, even your religious or spiritual outlook."*

What does this mean for people like us — leaders, entrepreneurs and those striving for more? It means that the beliefs we allow to linger unchecked are shaping not just our careers, but our happiness, relationships and personal growth. It's easy to assume that once you've reached a certain level of success, these mental barriers disappear but in reality, even the most seasoned leaders and entrepreneurs aren't immune to limiting beliefs. These mental barriers can quietly erode your confidence, making decisions more difficult and causing you to hold back from seizing opportunities that could take you to the next level.

That's why it's crucial to remain aware of the words and thoughts we allow to shape our beliefs. Are we telling ourselves we're not deserving of success? That being happy while being successful is too much to ask for?

HOW BELIEFS SHAPE SUCCESS AND HAPPINESS

There's a powerful sequence at work: thoughts lead to beliefs, beliefs shape the mindset, mindset drives actions, and actions determine your results.

This idea aligns closely with the concept explored in Maxwell Maltz's groundbreaking book, Psycho-Cybernetics. Maltz explains that the human brain and nervous system function like a goal-seeking machine, much like a guided missile or a computer, continuously working towards the objectives it has been programmed with. This "servo-mechanism" is driven by the mental images and beliefs we hold about ourselves, which directly influence our actions and behaviours. Positive, constructive programming fosters success, while limiting beliefs can lead to self-sabotage or being trapped in unproductive patterns. By consciously reprogramming this internal "mental blueprint" through techniques like visualisation and setting clear goals, Maltz demonstrates how we can harness the brain's natural mechanisms to achieve personal and professional success with precision and purpose

If you're not mindful of the thoughts you're entertaining daily, you could be unknowingly holding yourself back from the breakthroughs you're capable of achieving. The path to sustainable success isn't just about having the right strategy or the best skills; it's about recognising and overcoming the limiting beliefs that have settled into your subconscious mind.

Here's an example: You might have a goal of becoming a highly successful entrepreneur. But if you've internalised the belief that "successful entrepreneurs work 24/7 and sacrifice their personal lives", you may find yourself either burnt out or procrastinating on your business because, deep down, you're not willing to make that trade-off. In that case, the limiting belief isn't just holding back your success — it's preventing you from being happy with the journey.

OVERCOMING LIMITING BELIEFS FOR SUSTAINABLE SUCCESS

The good news? Limiting beliefs don't have to control you forever. With the right tools, you can identify, challenge and replace these beliefs with new ones that support your goals for both success and happiness.

We've already introduced the Quantum Release Method™, which is one of the fastest ways to release these limiting beliefs and align your mindset with your goals. But before you can release these beliefs, you need to identify them.

Start by asking yourself:

- "What do I believe about success?"
- "Do I believe that success requires sacrifice? If so, what sacrifices do I think I need to make?"
- "What do I believe about happiness? Can I be both successful and happy?"
- "Do I feel worthy of both success and happiness or do I feel I have to choose one over the other?"

Identifying these core beliefs is the first step toward dismantling them. Once you see them for what they are — just thoughts, not facts — you can begin to challenge them.

CHALLENGING LIMITING BELIEFS

How can we challenge these deeply ingrained beliefs?

One of the most effective tools is focused awareness—the practice of being fully present with your thoughts and feelings, without judgment. When limiting beliefs arise, instead of accepting them automatically, focused awareness allows you to pause and examine them.

For instance, if you catch yourself thinking, "Success always comes at a cost," take a moment to ask, "Is this truly the case?" You may realise there are countless examples of people who have built successful careers while maintaining fulfilling personal lives. In that moment, you create space to replace the limiting belief with one that serves you better, such as, "I can create success that enhances my happiness, not detracts from it."

As mentioned earlier, the brain is an evidence-seeking machine. The more evidence you provide to support your new belief, the stronger it becomes. To accelerate this process, actively search for examples—no matter how small—that reinforce the truth of your new belief. Think of yourself as a detective, gathering evidence to build a case for the belief that supports your desired outcome.

The next crucial step is to take **bold** action. Shifting your mindset isn't enough; you need to act in alignment with your new beliefs. Take meaningful steps that affirm your new perspective and bring you closer to the vision of success and happiness you're striving for.

Beliefs, thoughts, feelings, emotions, **and** visualisation form a powerful feedback loop that shapes our reality. Beliefs lay the foundation, influencing the thoughts we entertain regularly. These thoughts trigger corresponding emotions and feelings, which shape how we perceive and respond to the world. By introducing visualisation into this equation, you're not just imagining a desired outcome; you're actively engaging your beliefs, thoughts, and emotions to create a new reality. Visualisation, when combined with strong, positive emotions, reinforces new beliefs and trains your brain to see that outcome as achievable—even inevitable. This alignment between belief and emotion amplifies the power of visualisation, helping to rewire your brain and drive actions that align with your goals, making success more attainable.

HEART AND BRAIN COHERENCE: THE KEY TO UNLOCKING POWERFUL VISUALISATION

When it comes to achieving your goals and reprogramming your subconscious mind, there's a concept that elevates your efforts to a whole new level — heart and brain coherence. This is the state in which your heart and brain work in harmony, creating an optimal emotional, mental and physical environment for success. When we talk about visualisation and emotions, coherence is the bridge that connects them, enhancing the power of both.

Heart-brain coherence goes beyond just thinking positively or imagining success; it's about synchronising your physiological and emotional states to achieve alignment. Research from the HeartMath Institute shows that the heart generates a much stronger electromagnetic field than the brain and this field directly influences how we think, feel and behave. In fact, the heart sends more signals to the brain than the brain sends to the heart. When these signals are harmonious, your entire system operates at its best — cognitively, emotionally and physically.

THE SCIENCE BEHIND HEART-BRAIN COHERENCE

When your heart and brain are in coherence, your body functions at its peak. You feel more focused, calm, and emotionally balanced. This state is characterised by smooth, ordered rhythms in your heart rate which, in turn, create a calming effect on the brain. Achieving coherence can transform your ability to visualise success, because when your body is in this state, the emotions you generate during visualisation are amplified. You're not just seeing success in your mind's eye — you're *feeling* it deeply in your body.

What's fascinating is that when you feel positive emotions like gratitude, joy or love, your heart rhythms become more ordered, which helps your brain enter a state of coherence. This emotional alignment boosts your ability to focus and enhances the effectiveness of your visualisation practice. It's one thing to visualise success, but when you link those visualisations to feelings of gratitude or excitement, you take the process to another level entirely. In this state, your body and mind are working together to create a powerful signal to your subconscious mind.

WHY EMOTIONS ARE KEY TO COHERENCE

Emotions are the driver of heart-brain coherence. Negative emotions like stress, anxiety or frustration create chaotic heart rhythms, which disrupt the brain's ability to think clearly and focus on goals. But when you intentionally generate positive emotions, you shift your heart rhythms into a more coherent state, which directly impacts your brain's ability to process information effectively.

When you practise visualisation in a state of heart-brain coherence, your brain and heart are working together to create the mental and emotional environment that makes achieving your goals feel natural and effortless. By visualising your desired outcome and attaching emotions like gratitude or joy to it, you're signalling to your brain that this is not just an imagined future — it's something that's already happening in your reality. Your brain doesn't fully distinguish between a vividly imagined experience and a real one, so these emotional visualisations create new neural pathways that reinforce the belief that your goals are within reach.

HOW TO CULTIVATE HEART-BRAIN COHERENCE

Here's how you can start practising heart-brain coherence to supercharge your visualisation process:

1. **Focus on Your Heart**: Begin by closing your eyes and bringing your attention to the area around your heart. Imagine your breath flowing in and out of your chest, as though you're breathing directly through your heart.

2. **Generate Positive Emotions**: Once you're focused on your heart, intentionally generate feelings of gratitude, love or joy. Think of a person, place or experience that brings you genuine happiness and focus on that feeling.
3. **Visualise Your Goal**: As you cultivate these positive emotions, start visualising your desired outcome. Imagine it in vivid detail and, as you do, allow the feelings of success and achievement to grow stronger. Picture yourself already living in that reality, with all the emotions that would come with it.
4. **Repeat Consistently**: Like any practice, consistency is key. The more often you engage in heart-brain coherence while visualising your goals, the more you'll train your brain to recognise and act on the opportunities that align with your vision.

LINKING COHERENCE TO SUSTAINABLE SUCCESS

By regularly practising heart-brain coherence, you're not only improving your mental and emotional state but also sending a clear signal to your subconscious mind. This state of alignment makes it easier to act in ways that support your goals and to remain resilient in the face of challenges. When your brain and heart are working together in harmony, your visualisations become more than just daydreams — they become a powerful tool for manifesting the success you seek.

Achieving heart-brain coherence unlocks a deeper level of emotional and mental focus, allowing you to tap into the full potential of your visualisations. When you link your visualisations to positive emotions, you create a state of flow where your goals start to feel not just possible, but inevitable. And that's the foundation of long-term, sustainable success.

SUSTAINABLE SUCCESS: THE JOURNEY AHEAD

The road to sustainable success doesn't have to be paved with sacrifice and dissatisfaction. By identifying and overcoming your limiting beliefs, you create space for both success and happiness to flourish in your life. These aren't mutually exclusive; they're intertwined, and one fuels the other.

Through focused awareness, the Quantum Release Method™ and a commitment to challenging limiting beliefs, you can shift your mindset to one that supports your growth, happiness and long-term success.

CHECKLIST FIVE CHECKLIST FOR IDENTIFYING AND CHALLENGING LIMITING BELIEFS

Identify Your Limiting Beliefs

- What do I believe about success?
- Do I believe that success requires sacrifice?
- What limiting beliefs do I have around happiness and success coexisting?

Practice Focused Awareness

- Become aware of limiting thoughts as they arise.
- Question the validity of these thoughts. Are they facts, or just beliefs?

Reframe Your Beliefs

- Replace limiting beliefs with empowering ones. For example, instead of "Success requires sacrifice", try "Success and happiness can coexist".

Use the Quantum Release Method™

- Implement the Quantum Release Method™ to release deeply rooted limiting beliefs quickly and effectively.

Take Bold Action

- Align your actions with your new beliefs.
- Celebrate small wins that reinforce your new mindset.

By taking these steps, you can release the limiting beliefs that block both your success and happiness and begin to experience sustainable success — the kind that allows you to thrive in all areas of life.

SECTION THREE

INCREASE YOUR CAPACITY FOR SUSTAINABLE SUCCESS

Success at a new level requires you to increase your capacity to hold that level. Many people achieve success only to lose it because they haven't developed the mental, emotional or physical resilience to sustain it. This section focuses on building your capacity — enhancing your ability to cope with greater responsibility, more opportunities and higher stakes without becoming overwhelmed. This is where you strengthen your foundation, so you're not just achieving success but maintaining it effortlessly.

6

THE POWER OF FLOW: SUCCESS WITHOUT THE GRIND

Now that you've defined your new vision, let's talk about how you're going to achieve it. Here's the best part: it's not about working harder. This involves leveraging aligned action and accessing the power of flow states.

ALIGNED ACTION: THE KEY TO UNLOCKING PURPOSEFUL PROGRESS

Aligned action is the bridge between your vision and reality. It's about ensuring that every step you take and every decision you make is in harmony with your values, goals and long-term aspirations. When your actions are aligned with who you are and where you want to go, progress doesn't feel forced or chaotic. It feels purposeful, steady and clear.

Many leaders fall into the trap of chasing goals that, while impressive on the surface, don't truly resonate with their core values. They focus on external metrics of success, like financial growth or status, without pausing to ask whether these pursuits align with their personal beliefs and deeper purpose. This disconnect can lead to burnout, frustration or a sense of emptiness, even after significant accomplishments.

Aligned action, however, ensures that your efforts not only drive success but also fulfilment. When your actions match your vision and values, you are more energised, motivated and resilient. Every decision, from the smallest task to the largest strategic move, feels intentional and in service of your broader mission.

UNDERSTANDING WHAT ALIGNMENT FEELS LIKE

Taking aligned action isn't just about doing what you think is right or what looks good on paper. It's about tuning into how your decisions feel. When you're in alignment, you'll notice a sense of ease, flow and purpose in what you do. There's a clarity that guides your choices and a sense of direction that keeps you grounded, no matter the challenges.

It's important to regularly check in with yourself and ask, "Does this action reflect my vision? Does it feel aligned with my core values?" When the answer is yes, you'll notice that even the hard work feels meaningful. Conversely, when you're misaligned, everything feels like an uphill battle, leading to frustration and exhaustion.

As a leader, taking aligned action has a ripple effect on your team, your business and your broader community. When you operate from a place of alignment, you inspire those around you to do the same. Your team will see the clarity in your decisions, the purpose behind your actions and the integrity in how you lead. This cultivates trust, motivation and a shared sense of purpose among those you work with.

Aligned leaders also create businesses that reflect their values. They don't just chase profits, they build cultures, relationships and strategies that feel in harmony with their vision. This alignment is often what leads to long-term, sustainable success because it fosters loyalty, innovation and a deeper connection with both employees and customers.

UNLOCKING YOUR FULL POTENTIAL THROUGH ALIGNMENT

The beauty of aligned action is that it creates exponential growth without burnout. When you align your actions with your values and vision, you tap into a well of inner strength, clarity and motivation. You no longer waste energy on things that don't matter. Instead, you focus on what truly moves the needle in both your personal fulfilment and professional success.

In the end, aligned action is about living a life and leading in a way that feels good, not just in the short term but over time. It's about knowing that the steps you take today are not only driving your success but also building a legacy that reflects who you truly are. With alignment, you move through life with a sense of purpose, resilience and clarity that keeps you on the path to your highest potential.

In the traditional mindset, we're often taught that relentless hard work — pushing harder and grinding longer — is the only way to reach success. While hard work certainly plays a role, there's a better, more sustainable way forward. It's about moving from hustle to flow.

Flow is a psychological state where you become fully immersed in an activity, losing all sense of time. Distractions fade, your focus sharpens and everything feels effortless. When you're in flow, you operate at your highest level of productivity but without the usual stress and exhaustion that come from forcing results. It's a state where success feels natural, not forced.

Flow isn't just a nice-to-have, it's a game-changer for high performance. Michael Jordan's legendary 1992 NBA Finals performance, where he made six three-pointers in one half, is one of the most famous examples of flow in action. Jordan was so locked into the moment that everything came together effortlessly. Even he couldn't explain it, which is why he famously shrugged after the sixth shot. It was pure flow.

Usain Bolt, the fastest man alive, has also described how his world-record-breaking races felt almost effortless when he was in flow. His body moved instinctively, his mind was clear and his performance peaked because he was in perfect sync with the moment. Bolt's results weren't about pushing harder but about being fully absorbed in the race.

The beauty of flow is that it's not reserved for athletes. You can reach this state of peak performance in your own career and life, and when you do, success becomes more efficient and satisfying. When you're in flow, you're not grinding — you're thriving.

THE SCIENCE OF FLOW: BOOSTING PERFORMANCE

Flow has been widely studied and the science behind it is fascinating. Psychologist, Mihaly Csikszentmihalyi, one of the pioneers in the study of flow, defined it as "the optimal experience". He found that people are at their happiest and most productive when they're in flow. In fact, studies show that people in flow states report higher levels of creativity, focus and satisfaction. Not only do you perform better in flow, but you also feel better doing it.

Research conducted by Harvard psychologist, Teresa Amabile, found that people are five times more productive when in flow compared to when they're not. This means that working in flow for just a few hours can yield more results than an entire day of grinding.

Neuroscience supports this too. During flow, your brain releases a cocktail of neurochemicals, including dopamine, endorphins and serotonin, which heighten focus and enhance creativity. The prefrontal cortex — the part of the brain responsible for self-criticism and doubt — temporarily shuts down, making it easier to take risks, think creatively and push boundaries without hesitation.

FLOW IN ACTION: STUDIES AND EXPERIMENTS

Studies have consistently demonstrated the power of flow in a variety of contexts. One notable experiment conducted by McKinsey & Company found that top executives in flow are five times more productive than when they're not. This means that achieving flow just one day a week could make you as productive as if you'd worked for five days straight.

In another study, conducted at the University of Chicago, participants were asked to report on their experiences of flow in their daily lives. The results showed that people who regularly experienced flow not only performed better but also reported higher levels of happiness and fulfilment. This highlights an important aspect of flow: it's not just about doing more; it's about doing better while feeling more connected to the work itself.

Flow isn't just about performance; it's about unlocking your full potential and creating a pathway to long-term, sustainable success. The more you practice entering flow, the easier it becomes to access it regularly, allowing you to operate at your peak without burning out.

FLOW AND VISUALISATION: STRENGTHENING THE LINK

Visualisation can also be a powerful tool to help you enter flow. When you visualise yourself successfully completing a task, your brain starts to build the neural pathways that make that success possible. This primes your mind for the real task, allowing you to enter flow more easily. Visualisation helps to bridge the gap between intention and action, preparing your brain to recognise and seize the flow state when the moment comes.

FLOW AND SUSTAINABLE SUCCESS

The beauty of flow is that it's sustainable. Unlike pushing yourself to the point of exhaustion, flow allows you to perform at your best without draining your energy. When you operate in flow, you achieve more with less effort and your work feels more meaningful. Flow isn't just about efficiency; it's about creating a deeper connection with your work and aligning with your highest potential.

By shifting from a grind mentality to a flow state, you're not only improving your performance but also setting yourself up for long-term, sustainable success. Flow helps you move through challenges with ease, stay focused on your goals and enjoy the process along the way.

In the chapters ahead, we'll dive deeper into how you can cultivate flow in different areas of your life and work. But for now, remember this: success doesn't have to be hard. When you align your goals, create the right conditions and allow yourself to enter flow, you unlock a level of achievement that feels effortless yet incredibly powerful. That's the key to thriving, not just surviving, on your journey to sustainable success.

THE SUCCESS SLIP LANE: WHERE FLOW MEETS EASE

Here's where the concept of the **Success Slip Lane** comes in. Think of flow as your fast lane to success – the place where things don't just get done; they get done easily, efficiently and with a sense of fulfilment. This is your "slip lane," where you can move forward rapidly without feeling the grind or exhaustion that typically accompanies hard work.

In the traditional hustle mentality, we're conditioned to believe that success requires constant effort and pushing against resistance. But in the **Success Slip Lane**, you're not grinding, you're gliding. It's the state where your ambition aligns perfectly with your capacity and you achieve your goals faster with far less friction.

The secret to the Success Slip Lane is learning how to enter flow states more consistently. The more time you spend in flow, the faster and more easily you'll achieve your goals. This doesn't mean you stop working hard; it means you're working *smarter*, aligning your tasks with your natural rhythms and operating at peak performance when it matters most.

THE SCIENCE OF SUCCESS: WHY FLOW WORKS

So, why does flow work so well? The answer lies in the way flow alters your brain's chemistry and function. When you're in flow, your brain releases neurochemicals like dopamine, norepinephrine, and anandamide. These chemicals enhance mood, focus, and creativity, allowing you to work at peak performance.

In fact, as mentioned before, studies have shown that people in flow are five times more productive than those who are not. That's why athletes, military professionals, and top business leaders all use flow to elevate their performance. They understand that flow isn't just a "nice-to-have"; it's an essential tool for achieving success more quickly, without burning out.

The **Success Slip Lane** isn't about working harder; it's about working in a way that feels effortless and aligned. It's about harnessing your brain's natural capabilities to reach a state of optimal performance without the stress and exhaustion of constant hustle. And the beauty of flow is that once you learn how to access it regularly, you'll find that success not only comes easier, but it also feels more fulfilling.

HOW TO CULTIVATE FLOW AND ENTER THE SUCCESS SLIP LANE

To get into flow more regularly, you need to create the right conditions. Flow isn't something that just happens; it's something you can actively cultivate. Here are the key elements to achieving flow and stepping into your **Success Slip Lane**:

1. **Set Clear Goals**: Flow requires clarity. You need to know exactly what you're trying to achieve at any given moment. Set specific, measurable goals for each task or project. The clearer your objectives, the easier it is for your brain to focus.
2. **Balance Challenge and Skill**: Flow happens when you're stretched just enough. If a task is too easy, you'll get bored. If it's too difficult, you'll get overwhelmed. The goal is to find the sweet spot where your skills are being tested but not to the point of stress.
3. **Minimise Distractions**: To enter flow, you need uninterrupted focus. Minimise distractions by turning off notifications, setting boundaries with colleagues or family members and creating a workspace that supports concentration. The more focused you are, the more easily you can slip into flow.
4. **Use Time Blocks**: One effective way to cultivate flow is through time blocking. Set aside dedicated blocks of time for deep work, where you focus entirely on one task without distractions. This trains your brain to enter flow more easily during those periods.
5. **Listen to Your Body and Mind**: Flow requires energy. If you're tired, stressed, or running on empty, it will be much harder to enter flow. Make sure you're taking care of your body and mind through regular breaks, proper nutrition and stress management techniques like meditation or breathwork.
6. **Embrace Failure as Feedback**: Flow thrives when you're willing to experiment and take risks. Don't be afraid to fail. See every setback as an opportunity to learn and improve. The more you embrace this mindset, the more freely you'll move into flow.

7. **Incorporate the Quantum Release Method™**: Finally, use tools like the Quantum Release Method™ to clear any mental blocks or limiting beliefs that might be stopping you from accessing flow. The Quantum Release Method™ helps you align your subconscious mind with your goals, making it easier to step into a state of effortless performance.

CHAPTER SIX CHECKLIST:
THE POWER OF FLOW: SUCCESS WITHOUT THE GRIND

Define Your Vision Clearly

- Ensure your vision is specific and deeply meaningful to you.
- Align your goals with your long-term vision, creating a roadmap that excites and inspires you.

Focus on Flow, Not Grind

- Shift your mindset from pushing harder to working smarter by accessing flow.
- Understand that peak performance comes when you're fully immersed, not overworking.

Set Up Conditions for Flow

- Set clear goals for each task and find the balance between challenge and skill.
- Minimise distractions by creating a focused, conducive work environment.
- Use time-blocking techniques to dedicate uninterrupted periods for deep work.

Utilise Visualisation Techniques

- Visualise yourself achieving success to activate your Reticular Activating System (RAS).
- Link your visualisations to positive emotions to enhance your ability to access flow.

Embrace the Success Slip Lane

- Cultivate the mindset that success doesn't have to be hard. It can be smooth and fulfilling.
- Use tools like the Quantum Release Method™ to clear mental blocks and align your subconscious with your goals.
- Stay consistent in accessing flow states to achieve sustainable, long-term success.

This checklist will help you move from grind to flow, increasing your capacity for success without burning out. Remember, the key is alignment between your goals, your vision and how you approach your work. When these are in harmony, success becomes inevitable and sustainable.

7

NERVOUS SYSTEM REGULATION FOR PEAK PERFORMANCE

We've talked a lot about strategy and planning, but none of that holds up when your nervous system is out of balance. It's the unseen force that can make or break your ability to achieve sustainable success. Think about those moments when stress and pressure seem to knock you completely off course — when you feel triggered and, no matter what you tell yourself, you can't seem to stop the spiral. This isn't just a bad day; it's your nervous system reacting, often unconsciously, to perceived threats or overwhelm.

If you've ever felt like you're stuck in a cycle of self-sabotage — whether it's procrastination, snapping at loved ones or even physical health issues — chances are your nervous system is playing a role. And this is where the conversation shifts from just focusing on external success strategies to looking inward. If your body's stress response is constantly firing, no amount of strategic planning or hard work will create lasting success. Sustainable achievement requires a nervous system that's balanced, resilient and able to navigate stress without derailing your progress.

THE ROLE OF THE NERVOUS SYSTEM IN SUCCESS

Your nervous system is your body's command centre. It governs how you respond to stress, challenges and opportunities. When it's regulated and balanced, you can move through life with clarity and focus, making decisions from a place of calm rather than chaos. But when your nervous system is in constant "fight or flight" mode, triggered by real or perceived threats, you become reactive, often without even realising it.

These reactions can be subtle, like snapping at a colleague over a minor issue, or more extreme, like burning out after pushing yourself too hard for too long. Either way, when your nervous system is dysregulated, it affects every area of your life: your work, your health, and your relationships.

TRIGGERS AND THE SPIRAL

We've all experienced those moments when something seemingly small sets off a chain reaction of stress, anger or anxiety. A missed deadline, a disagreement with a partner or even something as simple as an unexpected email can send you into a spiral. What's frustrating is that these triggers are often completely unconscious. They bypass your logical brain and hit you straight in your emotional core, making it hard to control your reactions.

When you're triggered, your body reacts as if it's under threat, even if the actual situation is relatively minor. Your nervous system kicks into overdrive, releasing stress hormones like cortisol and adrenaline. Your heart rate increases, your breathing becomes shallow, and your body prepares for a fight—even though there's nothing to physically fight. Over time, these constant stress responses can take a toll on your health, leading to exhaustion, chronic anxiety or even more severe health issues.

The impact isn't just physical, though, it's emotional and relational too. You might find yourself snapping at loved ones, feeling disconnected or struggling to communicate effectively when you're stressed. These triggers can push you into cycles of self-doubt, affecting your ability to maintain strong relationships and make sound decisions, which are both essential for long-term success.

WHY MASTERING NERVOUS SYSTEM REGULATION IS ESSENTIAL

If you're serious about achieving sustainable success, nervous system regulation is not just a "nice to have", it's essential. Without it, you'll constantly find yourself on the back foot, reacting to situations rather than responding thoughtfully. This leads to burnout, strained relationships and, ultimately, an inability to maintain your success.

When your nervous system is regulated, you can handle stress and pressure without being thrown off course. You can think clearly, make better decisions and recover more quickly from setbacks. Nervous system mastery allows you to step out of the reactive cycle and into a space of calm control, where you can lead with confidence and resilience.

THE IMPACT ON HEALTH AND RELATIONSHIPS

Chronic stress, triggered by an unregulated nervous system, is directly linked to a wide range of health problems, from digestive issues to weakened immune systems to mental health disorders like anxiety and depression. When your body is in a constant state of fight or flight, it doesn't have the energy or resources to maintain optimal health.

But it's not just your health that suffers. Your relationships take a hit as well. An unregulated nervous system makes it difficult to communicate effectively, manage conflict or show up fully for the people you care about. You may find yourself snapping at loved ones, withdrawing emotionally or feeling disconnected from those around you. The strain of these emotional reactions, when left unchecked, can damage even the strongest relationships, leaving you isolated just when you need support the most.

EXPANDING OUR ENERGETIC SET POINTS TO INCREASE OUR CAPACITY FOR SUCCESS

Let's dig deeper into something that often gets overlooked – your energetic set points. In *The Big Leap*, Gay Hendricks talks about the "upper limit problem," where we all have an invisible ceiling that caps how much success, love or happiness we allow ourselves. We might consciously push for more, but if our nervous system isn't aligned with that new level, we'll unconsciously pull back the moment we start to approach it.

Have you ever hit a major goal and suddenly felt anxious or like you don't belong? That's your energetic set point talking, trying to keep you "safe". To grow and hit higher levels of success, you need to expand those set points and build the capacity to handle more.

RECOGNISING LIMITING PATTERNS

We've all got patterns and when they keep coming back to bite us, it's infuriating.

For example, think about your financial habits. Maybe every time you make a big financial leap, whether it's saving more, earning a higher income or paying off debt, you find yourself slipping back. You've been working hard, but somehow you're back in the same spot, like you're playing financial whack-a-mole. This is your energetic set point keeping you in your comfort zone, where things feel "normal", even if that normal is holding you back.

I've been there, too. For years, I had a pattern in relationships. Just when things were going well, I'd create drama or distance, as if my system couldn't handle the idea of deep intimacy. I'd push people away and then wonder why I kept ending up in shallow, unsatisfying relationships.

And then there was my business. The first time I received a large payment — an amount that would've been my yearly salary just a few years earlier — I didn't know what to do with myself. Consciously, I was excited, but my nervous system went haywire. I got so stressed I ended up in bed for a week with the flu! My system wasn't ready to handle that level of success. Sound familiar?

Another common set point many of us face is with body weight and fitness. You follow a strict routine, hit your target and then, boom! You're back at your old habits, gaining the weight back or losing the fitness you worked so hard for. It's like something inside pulls you back to where you started.

Here's why: energetic set points exist as a safety mechanism. Our subconscious doesn't operate on logic, it operates on survival. Anything unfamiliar, whether it's success, more money or a better body, can trigger fear because it represents change. And change, in the eyes of our primitive brain, can be dangerous.

Reflect on your own life. Do you notice patterns that keep you from moving forward? Recognising these patterns is the first step towards breaking free from them.

THE LEADERSHIP BALANCING ACT: STRATEGY MEETS NERVOUS SYSTEM REGULATION

We've all heard that strategy sets the course, but it's self-regulation that keeps you steady when the pressure mounts. Leadership isn't just about making decisions — it's about staying sharp, calm, and adaptable when the heat is on. And the key to that lies in how well you manage your nervous system.

Leadership roles are demanding. We're juggling high-stakes decisions, team dynamics and the constant need for innovation. All of this requires us to maintain resilience, clarity and composure. What's often overlooked is how closely these abilities are tied to the nervous system — your body's internal command centre. When we talk about sustainable success, we're talking about balance — an internal equilibrium that allows you to perform at your peak while recovering effectively between bouts of intense pressure.

In leadership, you're constantly walking the tightrope between sympathetic drive (the fight-or-flight response that keeps you on alert) and parasympathetic recovery (the rest-and-digest state that helps you restore and recharge). When this balance is out of whack, everything suffers — your decision-making, your health and your ability to lead effectively. So, regulating your nervous system isn't just a wellness trend, it's a performance strategy for fine-tuning leadership effectiveness.

UNDERSTANDING YOUR AUTONOMIC NERVOUS SYSTEM

Our brains and bodies are highly reactive, more than most of us realise. You might think your surroundings only impact your thoughts and feelings, but they trigger a cascade of physiological responses that affect how you function day-to-day.

Consider this: you can consciously control movements, like lifting a coffee cup or walking into a room, but your autonomic nervous system (ANS) manages the processes you can't consciously control, like your heartbeat, digestion and pupil dilation. While we don't directly control it, we're constantly feeding it cues that shape how it operates. And it responds in three to five seconds — that's how fast the body reacts to your environment.

At its core, the ANS operates as your body's internal regulator, keeping you in balance. It governs everything from your organs to your emotions and its primary job is to balance two opposing forces: the sympathetic and parasympathetic nervous systems. One keeps you on high alert and the other brings you back to a state of calm. When they're in harmony, that's when you perform at your best.

But the reality of modern leadership often disrupts this balance, leading to a host of negative consequences, such as mental fog, burnout or even chronic health issues. Understanding how these systems work can be a game-changer for anyone serious about peak performance.

SYMPATHETIC VS. PARASYMPATHETIC: THE LEADERSHIP BALANCING ACT

Your sympathetic nervous system (SNS) is often called the fight-or-flight system. It's there to mobilise energy, sharpen focus, and help you respond to immediate threats. When you're in a high-stakes meeting, making critical decisions or navigating a crisis, that's your sympathetic system kicking into gear. It's your go-to for quick thinking and decisive action.

The SNS gets activated during the Four Es:

- Excitement
- Emergency
- Exercise
- Embarrassment

However, constant engagement of the sympathetic system without adequate downtime becomes problematic. This is where the parasympathetic nervous system (PNS) steps in. Often called the "rest-and-digest" system, the PNS is what allows you to recover, recharge and build resilience. It's activated during moments of relaxation, helping the body heal, grow and regain emotional stability. It's like your body's natural reset button.

Think of high-performing leaders who schedule deliberate downtime after major projects. They might take a few days off after a big launch and go hiking or just unplug. That's them consciously engaging their parasympathetic system to recover from stress and prepare for the next big challenge.

Leadership requires oscillation — a balance between taking decisive action (sympathetic activation) and allowing yourself to recover (parasympathetic activation). This constant rhythm between action and recovery is what keeps you at your best, both in the short-term and for the long haul.

RECOGNISING WHEN YOUR NERVOUS SYSTEM IS OUT OF BALANCE

Here's how to tell if your nervous system is out of sync:

1. **Odd Triggers**: You find yourself reacting to things that wouldn't normally bother you, like snapping at someone over a small issue or feeling overly frustrated about minor setbacks. These unexpected triggers are a sign your sympathetic system is on overdrive.
2. **Constant Tension**: You feel physically tense — tight shoulders, a clenched jaw or a stiff neck. This is your body bracing for stress, even when you think you're relaxed.
3. **Feeling Drained After Success**: You've just hit a major milestone, but instead of feeling energised, you feel completely wiped out. That's your nervous system struggling to cope with the new demands.
4. **Heightened Emotional Responses**: Everything feels a little too intense. Small problems feel overwhelming and it takes longer to bounce back from setbacks.

When you're stuck in sympathetic dominance — where the fight-or-flight response stays switched on — you'll eventually burn out. Without activating the parasympathetic system, your body doesn't get the rest it needs to restore itself, leading to chronic stress and poor decision-making.

EXPANDING YOUR CAPACITY: HOW TO SHIFT YOUR ENERGETIC SET POINTS

We've touched on the concept of energetic set points before, but here's how it plays out in practice. Set points are the invisible limits your nervous system places on your capacity for success and happiness. These are what make you feel uncomfortable when you start to stretch beyond your usual achievements—whether that's earning more money, gaining influence, or building deeper relationships. To expand these limits, you need to train your nervous system to handle more.

1. **Visualisation to Increase Capacity**
   Once again, a powerful method to expand your capacity to receive is through visualisation. Imagine receiving more of what you desire—whether it's financial abundance, love, or another goal. Push past the point of comfort by visualising this abundance doubling, then doubling again, far beyond what feels familiar. For example, imagine earning an income far greater than you've ever experienced or being surrounded by deeper love and connection. This process stretches your internal "muscle" and trains your nervous system to normalise greater levels of success and fulfilment. Because the subconscious mind doesn't differentiate between imagined scenarios and reality, with consistent practice, this new level will feel completely natural both internally and as you begin to experience changes externally.

2. **Cold Therapy: Resetting the Nervous System**
   Cold therapy is a simple yet effective way to reset your nervous system. Whether it's a cold shower, splashing cold water on your face, or immersing your face in ice water, this practice stimulates the vagus nerve and activates the parasympathetic system, calming your body. Begin with 30 seconds of cold exposure at the end of your shower and gradually increase over time. This technique not only reduces stress hormones but also boosts energy and strengthens your resilience to discomfort.
3. **Breath-Based Protocols: Managing Stress in Real-Time**
   Breathwork is another essential tool for regulating your nervous system. Techniques like box breathing (inhale for 4 counts, hold for 4, exhale for 4, hold for 4) and coherence breathing (5–6 slow breaths per minute) are particularly effective. These practices help to slow your heart rate, calm your mind, and manage stress in high-pressure moments. Incorporating breathwork into your daily routine ensures you can use it instinctively when stress arises.

EXPANDING ENERGETIC SET POINTS

Your set points limit how much success and happiness you feel comfortable receiving. To raise them, you must train your nervous system to handle more. By using tools like visualisation, cold therapy, and breathwork, you can recondition yourself to normalise higher levels of achievement and joy. Imagine surpassing your current limits within your visualisation practice, visualising yourself thriving in a space that once felt impossible. Over time, this shifts your internal capacity and reshapes your external reality.

CHAPTER SEVEN CHECKLIST FOR SHIFTING MENTAL AND EMOTIONAL STATES

1. Recognise the Need for a Shift

- Notice signs of stress, overwhelm, or discomfort.
- Identify whether you need to calm, refocus, or energise yourself.

2. Choose Your Strategy

- Cold Therapy: Use cold showers or facial immersion for instant reset.
- Breathwork: Practise box or coherence breathing for calming effects.
- Physical Cues: Use grounding techniques, like holding a textured object.

3. Visualisation for Capacity Building

- Imagine receiving greater levels of abundance, love, or success.
- Push past internal limits until the new level feels comfortable.

4. Tune Into Your Body

- Map where stress manifests physically (e.g., tight shoulders).
- Use stretching or movement to release tension.

5. Move to Reset

- Engage in a physical activity like yoga, stretching, or walking.
- Use movement to shift your mental and emotional state.

6. Make It a Regular Practice

- Incorporate these techniques daily to build mental and emotional resilience.
- Practise shifting during low-stress moments to prepare for high-pressure situations.

By mastering these strategies, you can expand your capacity to receive, reset your nervous system, and take bold action towards your goals. Over time, you'll unlock new levels of success, resilience, and fulfilment, allowing you to thrive beyond limits you once thought impossible.

8

OVERCOMING PROCRASTINATION AND INCREASING MOTIVATION

When we're working to raise our energetic set points, pushing ourselves to a higher level of performance and fulfilment, procrastination often sneaks in. Instead of focusing on what's truly important, we find ourselves filling time with distractions and avoiding the tasks that would move us forward. This behaviour only adds to a sense of unsustainability, pulling us away from the very goals we set out to achieve.

Procrastination in this context isn't just about delay; it's about misdirecting our energy. We pour effort into trivial tasks, keeping busy but not productive, and that drains our ability to focus on what truly matters. It becomes a cycle of avoidance, with energy scattered across meaningless activities, which not only slows our progress but also creates a sense of imbalance and burnout.

Breaking free from this cycle is essential for creating sustainable success. By recognising when procrastination is creeping in and redirecting our energy towards purposeful action, we can increase our capacity to operate at a higher level. Procrastination isn't just a productivity issue, it's an energy drain that undermines your growth. The key is learning to work with your energy, not against it, by focusing on what truly drives progress and fulfilment.

Procrastination is like being caught in a strong current. The more you resist or fight against it, the harder it becomes to move. But once you find your stroke and start swimming with purpose, the current no longer pulls you back, it becomes something you can work with. The trick is finding that flow — your momentum — and letting it carry you forward.

The following processes are designed to help you leverage the power of your unconscious mind to move forward with greater ease and clarity. As you now know, our unconscious mind plays a significant role in driving our behaviour, often steering us towards habits or distractions without us realising it. By tapping into its potential, you can align your actions with your goals, breaking free from the cycle of procrastination and creating sustainable progress.

These methods are about more than just "getting things done", they're about shifting your mindset and using your brain's natural processes to work for you, not against you. By engaging your unconscious mind, you can move past mental blocks and resistance, allowing your actions to flow more naturally towards the outcomes you desire.

DRIVING THROUGH PROCRASTINATION

Procrastination isn't laziness or a lack of discipline; it's often rooted in how the unconscious mind perceives certain actions. While understanding the root cause of procrastination can be helpful, spending excessive time analysing it isn't always productive. Instead, we can work with what we know about the unconscious mind to override the cycle of delay.

The unconscious mind tags actions as "safe" or "unsafe" based on our consistent behaviours. If we repeatedly move towards or away from something, the brain learns to categorise it accordingly. For example, take someone who smokes. Consciously, they know it's harmful, but they still associate it with calming down. Why? Because, over time, their brain has linked the act of smoking with safety, even though it triggers the same physiological responses as anxiety. The repeated action has overridden logic and built a sense of comfort.

Similarly, if you consistently avoid a task, your brain starts tagging that action as "unsafe," even if it's beneficial for you. The challenge then becomes retraining the brain to associate the task with safety. This means taking small, deliberate actions towards what you want to achieve, signalling to your brain that it's not only safe but rewarding. Over time, as you take consistent steps, your brain will rewire and start tagging the task as "safe," making it easier to overcome procrastination and build momentum.

To help the brain start tagging tasks as "safe," it's essential to take consistent, intentional steps towards them, retraining your mind to associate them with positive outcomes. For example, imagine you're procrastinating on writing a book. The idea of completing an entire manuscript might feel overwhelming, triggering avoidance. The same principle applies to other goals, like starting a fitness routine or preparing for a major presentation. Here's how to break through that resistance and build momentum:

BREAK THE TASK INTO MANAGEABLE PIECES

When you're faced with a large project, such as writing a book, it's easy to feel paralysed by the sheer scope of the task. This sense of overwhelm often leads to avoidance because the brain overestimates the difficulty of large goals. The solution is to break the task into smaller, more manageable pieces. For writing a book, start with an outline, then focus on writing just one paragraph or section at a time. If it's fitness, commit to a 10-minute workout instead of planning an hour-long session. Each small step reduces the psychological burden, making progress feel achievable and building momentum as you complete each piece.

START WITH THE TWO-MINUTE RULE

The hardest part of any task is often starting. The Two-Minute Rule helps lower the barrier to entry by committing to just two minutes of focused work. For example, if you're struggling to begin a chapter of your book, tell yourself you'll write for just two minutes. If you're avoiding preparing a presentation, commit to opening the slides and adding one idea. This small action often leads to more, as getting started makes it easier to keep going. The key is reducing mental resistance and allowing momentum to carry you forward.

SET CLEAR, ACHIEVABLE DEADLINES

Procrastination thrives when timelines are vague or non-existent. For example, if you tell yourself, "I'll write the book someday," or "I'll get to the gym eventually," there's no urgency. Instead, set clear, realistic deadlines. Commit to writing 500 words by the end of the day or finishing your first chapter by the weekend. Deadlines give your brain a sense of direction and accountability, ensuring that tasks don't remain open-ended. Make the deadlines challenging but realistic, so they push you to act without overwhelming you.

BUILD MOMENTUM WITH SMALL WINS AND TIMED SESSIONS

Momentum is a powerful antidote to procrastination. Start by stacking small wins. For example, completing a single paragraph or a 10-minute brainstorm for your book can create a sense of achievement that motivates further action. Using timed sessions, such as the Pomodoro Technique, can also be incredibly effective. Set a timer for 15 or 20 minutes and focus entirely on the task. Knowing there's a defined endpoint makes it easier for the brain to engage fully. Whether it's writing or another goal, these small bursts of focused work help you build momentum and reduce the tendency to avoid the task.

VISUALISE THE BENEFITS OF COMPLETING THE TASK

When motivation wanes, it's often because we focus on the effort involved rather than the rewards. Shift your attention to the benefits. For example, imagine the pride and satisfaction of holding your completed book in your hands or the confidence boost of delivering a successful presentation. Visualising the positive outcomes activates your brain's reward system, making the task feel more worthwhile and motivating you to take action. This strategy can also apply to personal goals, like imagining how energised and accomplished you'll feel after a workout.

By incorporating these techniques, you'll not only retrain your brain to see tasks as safe but also create a sustainable system for overcoming procrastination. Each step—no matter how small—builds confidence and momentum, helping you move steadily towards your goals.

GET OVER IT AND MOVE ON

Procrastination can lead to feelings of guilt or frustration, which often feeds back into the cycle of avoidance. The key to breaking this pattern is self-compassion. Forgive yourself for past procrastination and focus on moving forward. Let go of the guilt. Focus on your next action, not on what you've delayed. Self-compassion helps to rebuild your motivation and keeps you moving forward without the weight of self-criticism.

Overcoming procrastination isn't about forcing yourself to work harder. It's about creating momentum and finding your rhythm. By understanding what holds you back, breaking tasks into smaller pieces and using tools like the Two-Minute Rule, clear deadlines and positive momentum, you'll move towards your goals with focus and energy.

CHAPTER EIGHT CHECKLIST FOR OVERCOMING PROCRASTINATION AND INCREASING MOTIVATION

Sustainable success isn't about sprinting to the finish. It's about consistently making progress, one step at a time, without burning out. When you work with yourself rather than against yourself, you'll find that success becomes not just achievable but sustainable.

Leverage Your Unconscious Mind to Overcome Procrastination

- Reflect on what's causing your procrastination. It could be fear, perfectionism or overwhelm.
- Address the underlying issue rather than just focusing on the surface symptoms.

Break Tasks into Manageable Pieces

- Divide large tasks into smaller, actionable steps.
- Focus on one small task at a time to reduce overwhelm and build momentum.

Use the Two-Minute Rule

- Commit to just two minutes of focused work on a task.
- Starting small lowers resistance, making it easier to continue once you begin.

Set Clear, Achievable Deadlines

- Establish specific, realistic deadlines to keep tasks from being delayed.
- Push yourself forward with deadlines that create urgency without overwhelming you.

Stack Small Wins and Use Timed Sessions

- Celebrate each small achievement to build positive momentum.
- Use timed sessions to fully focus on a task for a set period, keeping your mind engaged and productive.

Visualise the Benefits

- Focus on the rewards of completing the task, not just the effort involved.
- Visualising success activates your brain's reward centres, boosting your motivation.

Forgive Yourself and Move On

- Let go of guilt over past procrastination and start fresh.
- Shift your focus to your next action, practising self-compassion to maintain progress.

9

BUILDING RESILIENCE FOR SUSTAINABLE SUCCESS

Resilience is the quiet powerhouse behind long-term success. It's not just about bouncing back from setbacks—it's about growing stronger through them. For people like us, living and leading in today's fast-paced and unpredictable world, resilience is the secret sauce. It's the skill that helps us adapt, learn, and innovate when things don't go to plan. In this chapter, we'll explore how resilience plays a key role in sustainable success and how we can build it to not just survive, but thrive.

WHY RESILIENCE MATTERS

Resilience isn't just about getting back on your feet after life knocks you down—it's about learning, growing, and coming back stronger. For people like us who are juggling big goals, careers, businesses, and families, resilience is the difference between staying stuck and moving forward. It's not about pushing through the pain with sheer willpower; it's about pivoting, adapting, and finding better ways to succeed.

Think about leaders we admire, like Howard Schultz of Starbucks. Back in 2008, Starbucks faced declining sales and store closures. Schultz didn't look for quick fixes to patch things up. Instead, he took bold, long-term action: retraining staff, improving customer experiences, and making tough decisions. He turned the adversity into an opportunity, and Starbucks came out stronger than ever.

THE SCIENCE OF RESILIENCE: HOW WE CAN GET STRONGER

Resilience isn't some mystical trait you're born with—it's backed by science, and it's something we can all develop. Studies show that resilient people are better at managing their emotions and staying optimistic, even under pressure. The good news? Resilience is a skill we can build, thanks to discoveries in neuroscience and genetics, like **neuroplasticity** and **epigenetics**.

- **Neuroplasticity**: This is the brain's ability to rewire itself in response to experiences. Every time we face a challenge and recover, our brain learns to handle stress better in the future. It's like building a mental muscle—the more we work it, the stronger it gets.
- **Epigenetics**: This is the science of how our environment and behaviours can influence which genes are "switched on" or expressed. By adopting resilient habits—like focusing on solutions, staying optimistic, and practising self-care—we're not just shifting our mindset; we're actually influencing our biological responses to stress.

These discoveries show us that resilience isn't just about enduring tough times—it's about evolving to handle them better. Every setback becomes an opportunity to grow stronger, mentally and physically.

When the heat is on, emotional resilience is what keeps us grounded. It's the ability to stay calm, clear, and composed when everything feels like it's falling apart.

But let's be real: staying calm isn't always easy. Stress and setbacks can knock us off our game. That's why emotional resilience isn't about avoiding those feelings—it's about training ourselves to respond thoughtfully instead of reacting impulsively.

Take **Sara Blakely**, the founder of Spanx, as an example. She faced countless rejections in the early days of her business. Instead of letting those setbacks crush her, she used them as fuel to keep going. Her optimism became her compass, helping her navigate the tough times and ultimately succeed.

WHEN THE WORST HAPPENS: BUILDING RESILIENCE IN REAL-TIME

It wouldn't be right to talk about resilience without addressing what to do when the proverbial "shit hits the fan." Challenges are **inevitable**. As leaders, this is the path we've chosen—one that demands navigating the unpredictable and facing adversity head-on. Life is going to throw curveballs; it's not a question of *if* but ***when***. The difference between being overwhelmed by setbacks and rising above them lies in how quickly and effectively we move through them.

For me, like many of you, the journey hasn't been without its fair share of trials. I've experienced the gut-punch of losing jobs I thought defined me, relationships I believed would last a lifetime, and even facing unprecedented business challenges, including court cases that came out of nowhere. On top of that, there have been health setbacks that hit like a freight train, knocking me flat. These moments hurt. They knock the wind out of your sails and make you question everything.

But here's the thing: our ability to claw our way back from these moments, adapt, and become stronger as a result is what sets us apart. It's what determines whether we move forward towards the life we want or crawl into a hole, giving up and accepting the lie that our dreams aren't meant for us. Resilience isn't about avoiding the pain; it's about refusing to let it define us.

FACING CHALLENGES: FROM CHAOS TO CLARITY

When something challenging happens, the most important thing we can do is get ourselves into a position to look at the situation objectively. In the heat of the moment, it can feel like the world is spinning out of control. Our natural reaction, as creatures wired for survival, is to assume the worst. Without intentional mental training, our minds will default to catastrophising: we think this is the last job we'll ever have, the last person who will ever love us, or the one mistake that ruins everything.

But here's the truth: the future is rarely as bleak as we imagine. If we look back at our lives, at the times when things didn't go as planned, we often see how those challenges redirected us to something better—opportunities we couldn't have imagined at the time. Even when it felt like the end of the world, in hindsight, it was often the beginning of something new.

That's where **The Resilient Leader Audio Programme** comes in. I designed this tool specifically to help leaders like you regain peace and alignment as quickly as possible when challenges hit. It's not about suppressing emotions but rather resetting your nervous system and removing the emotional charge from situations in record time. This programme helps you take the emotion out of the equation, allowing you to view things objectively and respond effectively.

You can find out more at *The Achievement Algorithm* website.

WHY RESILIENCE SETS US APART

For people like us, resilience is what gives us the edge. It's not about avoiding challenges—it's about handling them better, faster, and more effectively than the rest. Every setback is a chance to learn, grow, and prove to ourselves that we're capable of more.

With tools like **The Resilient Leader Audio Programme**, we can ensure that we're not just surviving challenges but thriving through them. Life will throw us obstacles, but resilience is what guarantees we get back up stronger, clearer, and ready for the next chapter.

CHAPTER NINE CHECKLIST FOR BUILDING RESILIENCE FOR SUSTAINABLE SUCCESS

Three Steps to Turn Challenges Into Growth

When life throws you a curveball, follow these steps to regain control and move forward:

1. Make Peace With Where You Are

The first step is acceptance. Fighting reality or wishing things were different won't change the situation. Instead, acknowledge what has happened and how you feel about it. This doesn't mean giving up or agreeing with the outcome—it means letting go of resistance so you can focus your energy on moving forward. Denial and blame only keep you stuck. Acceptance, on the other hand, creates the mental clarity needed to take the next step.

Example: If you lose an important client or job, don't waste energy beating yourself up or blaming external circumstances. Acknowledge the loss, allow yourself to feel disappointed, and then refocus on what's next.

2. Edge Forward From There

Once you've made peace with the situation, take one small, deliberate step forward. You don't have to fix everything at once—just take the next step that feels manageable. It could be sending out one job application, reaching out to a mentor for advice, or taking a moment to write down your thoughts and create a plan. These small actions build momentum and start to shift your mindset from defeat to possibility.

Example: After a personal setback, it might feel overwhelming to imagine starting over. Instead of focusing on the enormity of the task, break it into smaller, actionable pieces. A single positive step can reignite your belief in your ability to move forward.

3. Apply the Belief That This Is Happening for a Reason

This step requires trust: trust that life is aligning you with where you're truly meant to be. Even when it feels unfair or uncertain, remind yourself that this challenge is part of a larger journey, one that's ultimately guiding you to growth and success. Adversity often forces us to uncover strengths, insights, and opportunities we wouldn't have pursued otherwise. Reframe the setback as redirection rather than failure. It's not easy, but it's transformative. When you can hold onto the belief that challenges happen for a reason, you shift from being a victim of circumstances to an active participant in shaping your future.

Example: When faced with a business setback, remind yourself that some of the most successful ventures were born from failure. This could be the push you need to pivot, innovate, or pursue an entirely new direction that aligns with your bigger goals.

10

THE ART OF SHIFTING QUICKLY

In the previous chapter, we explored resilience — the ability to recover from setbacks and grow stronger in the face of adversity. But resilience isn't just about enduring challenges over time; it's about how quickly we can return to balance and regain control in the midst of those challenges. In other words, our power lies in our ability to shift back into homeostasis as swiftly as possible.

In high-pressure situations, when stress levels spike, our bodies instinctively react in ways that aren't always helpful. We enter a heightened state of awareness, where blood flow is redirected from the brain to other areas of the body — like the legs to run fast or the jaw to bite. While this might have served our ancestors well in life-threatening situations, it leaves modern-day leaders at a disadvantage. We become physically stronger but mentally weaker.

In this state, we lose access to our cognitive functionality — our ability to think logically, tap into intuition, focus deeply and solve problems with strategy and clarity. This is why stress-induced reactions can often lead to poor decision-making. When we're caught in the fight-or-flight response, we're no longer thinking like strategic leaders. We're just reacting.

What if, instead of getting stuck in this reactive state, you could train yourself to shift quickly? To return to calm, focus and clarity in moments of stress? This is not only possible but necessary for sustainable success in today's fast-paced world.

THE IMPORTANCE OF SHIFTING QUICKLY

In leadership and life, unexpected situations will arise and stress is inevitable. The real test of your effectiveness as a leader isn't about avoiding stressful situations, it's about how quickly you can bounce back, recalibrate and continue making strategic decisions. The longer you stay in that heightened, stressed-out state, the more likely you are to make decisions driven by panic rather than purpose.

Take a moment to think of the times when stress has clouded your judgment. Perhaps you've had a meeting where emotions ran high, or maybe you faced a critical deadline and found yourself overwhelmed by pressure. In those moments, did you find yourself reacting impulsively or making decisions you later regretted? That's because when you're in a state of heightened stress, your brain is not functioning at its peak capacity.

The goal of this chapter is to help you master the art of shifting quickly — moving from a reactive state of stress back to a place of calm, focus and control. We're going to cover some solid, actionable strategies that will allow you to regain your cognitive abilities in stressful moments, empowering you to think clearly and lead effectively.

WHY STRESS MAKES US "STUPID"

Let's break down why stress affects us the way it does.

When we perceive a threat, our brain triggers the fight-or-flight response, releasing hormones like adrenaline and cortisol. These chemicals prepare our bodies for physical action: our heart rate increases and blood is directed to large muscle groups, preparing us to either flee or defend ourselves. This survival mechanism is great if we're facing a physical threat but it's less useful when the threat is a deadline or a difficult conversation.

In these moments, we experience what is often referred to as "amygdala hijack". This is when the emotional part of the brain (the amygdala) overrides the logical, thinking part (the prefrontal cortex). This is why we say stress makes us "stupid", because, in these moments, we lose access to higher-order cognitive functions like problem-solving, creativity and rational decision-making. The blood that normally supports these functions has been diverted to the body's survival systems.

This is where learning how to shift quickly becomes critical. The faster you can calm your nervous system and bring your body out of this reactive state, the sooner you can regain access to your cognitive abilities and get back to making smart, strategic decisions.

In the following sections, we will give you some solid and actionable strategies for shifting quickly.

BRAINWAVE MODULATION FOR INSTANT FOCUS OR RELAXATION

We've touched on basic tools like deep breathing and mindfulness in earlier chapters, but when it comes to shifting quickly, **brainwave modulation** takes things to another level. This technique involves using specific frequencies to influence your brain's natural rhythms, allowing you to tap into different **brainwave states** depending on what you need in the moment, whether it's calming your nerves or sharpening your focus. It's like having a mental gear shift that you can control.

THE SCIENCE OF BRAINWAVES

Your brain operates on electrical impulses, and these impulses generate different brainwave frequencies, each linked to specific mental states. These brainwave patterns can be divided into five key types: Delta, Theta, Alpha, Beta and Gamma. Each state corresponds to different levels of consciousness and mental activity.

Here's a breakdown of the most relevant brainwave states for quickly shifting your mindset:

- **Alpha Waves (8-12 Hz)**: Alpha waves are associated with a **calm, relaxed state,** the kind of mental space you might experience during light meditation or just before falling asleep. When you're in the alpha state, you're more likely to feel stress-free, at ease and open to creative insights. If you've just come out of a tense situation or need to unwind after a long day, tapping into alpha waves helps you regain balance and **relieve stress**. This state is perfect for **relaxation and creative problem-solving**.
- **Beta Waves (13-30 Hz)**: Beta waves are linked to **active, alert thinking** and **focused concentration**. This is your brain's natural state when you're working through a task, making decisions or engaging in a conversation. While the beta state is necessary for productivity and performance, staying in high beta for too long can lead to feelings of anxiety or stress. The key is to **access beta waves when you need to focus**, then shift out of them when it's time to relax.
- **Gamma Waves (30-100 Hz)**: Gamma waves are the fastest of the brainwave states and are connected to **peak cognitive performance**. When your brain is in the gamma state, it's processing information at an incredible speed, making connections between ideas, and solving problems. This state is associated with moments of deep insight, creativity and learning. If you need to enhance mental clarity or break through a complex problem, gamma waves are what you're aiming for.

HOW BRAINWAVE MODULATION WORKS

So, how do you tap into these brainwave states on demand? This is where **binaural beats** come in. Binaural beats work by presenting two slightly different frequencies to each ear. For example, if you listen to a 300 Hz tone in your left ear and a 310 Hz tone in your right ear, your brain perceives the difference between these two tones and creates a third frequency, in this case, 10 Hz, which aligns with the **alpha brainwave range**. This process, called **brainwave entrainment**, encourages your brain to follow the frequency it perceives, guiding you into the desired state.

HOW TO USE BRAINWAVE MODULATION

Brainwave modulation is incredibly simple to incorporate into your routine, making it an accessible and powerful tool for quick mental shifts.

1. **Choose Your Frequency**: Decide which brainwave state you need. If you're feeling stressed and need to relax, choose a frequency that aligns with **alpha waves**. If you need to focus or boost productivity, go for a **beta wave** frequency. For those moments where you need a surge of mental clarity or creative insight, tap into **gamma waves**.
2. **Use Noise-Cancelling Headphones**: For maximum effect, it's important to listen through noise-cancelling headphones. This ensures that the binaural beats are delivered clearly without interference from external noise, allowing your brain to lock onto the frequency.

3. **Create the Right Environment**: Set yourself up in a quiet space where you won't be interrupted. Whether you're using brainwave modulation to focus or relax, the more you can minimise distractions, the quicker you'll feel the shift.
4. **Pair It With Breathwork**: To supercharge the effect, combine brainwave modulation with **deep breathing exercises**. Spend ten or fifteen minutes listening to the binaural beats while focusing on slow, controlled breathing. This not only helps you synchronise your brainwaves but also engages your parasympathetic nervous system, which promotes relaxation and mental clarity.

REAL-WORLD APPLICATIONS

Let's say you're about to step into an important meeting and your mind is racing, making it hard to focus. You've got ten minutes to centre yourself. Pop on your headphones, select a **beta wave frequency** to boost your alertness and spend a few minutes listening while doing deep breathing. By the time you walk into the room, your mind will be sharper and you'll feel more present and focused.

Or imagine you've had a stressful day and you're finding it hard to unwind. In this case, you'd choose an **alpha wave frequency** to help shift your brain into a calm, relaxed state. Combined with some light breathing or meditation, you'll feel the tension melt away, making it easier to decompress and enjoy your evening.

WHY IT WORKS

What makes brainwave modulation so effective is its **scientific foundation**. Your brain is highly adaptable and its electrical activity can be influenced by external stimuli like sound. By introducing these precise frequencies through binaural beats, you can guide your brain into the mental state you need within minutes, rather than waiting for it to happen naturally. It's a fast, reliable way to shift your mindset when time is of the essence.

Whether you need to **calm your nerves** before a big presentation, **focus your mind** on an important task, or **spark creativity** for a new project, brainwave modulation gives you the tools to access these states on demand. It's the kind of mental flexibility that keeps you sharp, balanced and able to adapt to any situation.

You can easily find binaural beats from a variety of sources and the best part is that they're readily accessible and simple to use. Music Streaming Services like Spotify, Apple Music and YouTube offer lots of different options, whether you're looking to relax, focus or spark creativity. Simply search for something like "alpha waves for relaxation" or "beta waves for focus" and you'll find plenty of options ready to use.

PHYSICAL CUES FOR A SENSORY RESET

When it feels like your mind is spiralling out of control, sometimes the quickest way to regain focus is by turning to your body. **Physical sensations** can have a powerful effect on your mental state. Think about it. Have you ever noticed how a hot shower after a stressful day seems to melt away tension or how squeezing a stress ball during a tough conversation helps you stay grounded? These sensory cues work because they give your brain something physical to focus on, helping you reset mentally.

Imagine you're in the middle of a chaotic workday — your inbox is overflowing, you've got back-to-back meetings and you can feel stress building up. In that moment, your mind is racing and you're struggling to concentrate. Instead of letting overwhelm take over, try this: grab a textured object such as a stress ball, a pen with a bumpy grip or even a piece of fabric and press it between your fingers. **Tactile pressure**, a subtle form of sensory grounding, has been shown to engage attention centres in the brain. It might sound simple, but that small physical action helps bring your mind back to the present, giving you a way to pause the chaos and regain clarity.

TEMPERATURE CONTRAST: A COOL (OR HOT!) RESET

Here's another quick hack — **temperature contrast**. It's something you probably do without even realising it. When athletes plunge into ice baths after an intense workout or sip hot tea on a freezing day, they're doing more than just managing their bodies, they're resetting their minds. You can do the same when stress hits.

Picture this: you're feeling anxious before a big presentation. Your heart's racing and your mind is scattered. Try holding a cold glass of water in your hand for a minute, then switch to a warm cup of coffee or tea. The **alternating temperature** engages your autonomic nervous system, which helps lower stress levels and shifts your brain out of panic mode. It's a simple technique that you can use anywhere, whether you're in the office, at home or even on the go.

NEUROLOGICAL ANCHORING: A SHORTCUT TO EMOTIONAL SHIFTS

Now, let's talk about **neurological anchoring**. This is a psychological trick used by high performers to instantly switch into a desired emotional state. Think of it as creating a mental "button" you can press when you need a boost of confidence or calmness. It's rooted in **Neuro-Linguistic Programming (NLP)**, a technique often used by top athletes and leaders.

A perfect example is **Tony Robbins**, who uses anchoring before stepping onto a stage to speak to thousands. He might do something as simple as clapping his hands or bouncing on his toes — a physical gesture that's deeply connected to a feeling of high energy and confidence. Every time he repeats the action, he triggers that emotional state. You can create your own anchors, too. Next time you're feeling at your best, whether it's during a workout, a great conversation or a moment of clarity, press your thumb and forefinger together. Keep doing this in moments of positivity and soon enough, this action becomes a mental shortcut to access that feeling when you need it most, like before a challenging meeting or presentation.

SOMATIC INTELLIGENCE: TUNING INTO YOUR BODY'S SIGNALS

We've all experienced those physical cues from our bodies — tight shoulders, a knot in your stomach or a pounding heart. These signals are your body's way of telling you that something's not quite right. But instead of pushing them aside, learning to **listen to your body** can be a game-changer.

Think of it like this: your body is your emotional compass. The next time you notice tension building up, take a moment to tune in. Is there tightness in your chest? Are your shoulders creeping up towards your ears? These physical sensations often show up before we even realise we're stressed. By recognising these cues early, you can stop stress from snowballing. This is where **somatic mapping** comes in. This is a technique that helps you identify where emotions show up in your body. Once you know where stress hits, you can respond quickly, whether that's through breathing exercises or a few stretches to release the tension.

MOVEMENT PRACTICES: SHIFTING STATE THROUGH ACTION

Movement has an incredible ability to shift your mental state. Whether it's **stretching, yoga or even a quick walk**, engaging your body helps release stored tension and allows you to reset mentally. Trauma expert, **Dr. Peter Levine,** developed somatic experiencing, a practice that combines movement with mindfulness to help people process and release stress. His research shows that when we allow our bodies to move and stretch, we release physical and emotional tension that, if left unchecked, can keep us feeling stuck.

Ever notice how a quick walk around the block clears your head? Or how a yoga session leaves you feeling refreshed and mentally sharp? That's the power of movement. Even something as simple as rolling your shoulders or standing up for a stretch can help reset your nervous system and shift you out of a stressed state.

MASTERING DE-ESCALATION: SHIFTING THE ATMOSPHERE AROUND YOU

Sometimes, shifting quickly isn't just about managing your own state, it's about managing the situation around you. In high-pressure environments, where emotions are running high, **de-escalation techniques** are vital for diffusing tension and keeping control of the room.

Think of **Nelson Mandela** during the height of South Africa's racial tensions. His calm demeanour and open body language often defused hostile situations before they escalated. By **modelling calmness** in your tone of voice, body language and energy, you can influence others to follow suit. People naturally mirror emotional states, so by staying steady, you encourage those around you to do the same.

Using empathetic language is another powerful tool. When emotions are running high, phrases like "I understand how you're feeling" can make all the difference. It shifts the focus from confrontation to collaboration, making it easier to steer the conversation towards resolution.

THE POWER OF QUICK SHIFTS FOR LONG-TERM SUCCESS

At the heart of all these techniques is one core principle: the faster you can **shift your mental and emotional state**, the quicker you can regain control and keep moving forward. Life is unpredictable and challenges will come your way but by mastering the art of quick shifts, whether through sensory cues, anchoring, or movement, you build a powerful resilience that keeps you balanced, composed, and ready for anything.

Success isn't about avoiding tough situations; it's about learning how to **navigate them with grace and confidence**.

By practising these quick-shift techniques, you'll be better equipped to handle whatever life throws your way, without falling back into old habits or losing your momentum.

RAPID TECHNIQUES FOR HANDLING HIGH-PRESSURE SITUATIONS

You've been there — the tension in a room is thick, emotions are running high and, as the leader, all eyes are on you to calm things down. In these moments, the ability to de-escalate the situation quickly is what sets effective leaders apart. Whether it's a heated argument in a meeting, a difficult negotiation or managing a team under stress, mastering the art of de-escalation is essential.

But here's the thing: it's not just about keeping your cool; it's about understanding how to use your presence, words and body language to lower the emotional temperature in the room. Let's explore how you can do this in a way that feels natural and effortless, even in the most intense situations.

THE POWER OF NON-THREATENING BODY LANGUAGE

Think about the last time someone snapped at you. How did their body language make you feel? Probably defensive, maybe even more upset. This is exactly what you want to avoid when things start to heat up. The first step in de-escalation is creating a non-threatening environment. This starts with your body language.

Here's how you can use your body to calm things down:

- **Keep an open stance**: Crossing your arms or standing too close to someone can feel confrontational. Stand with your arms relaxed and keep some distance to give the other person space. This signals that you're not a threat.
- **Relax your posture**: Tension shows and when you're tense, others feel it. Relax your shoulders, keep your posture open and take deep breaths to maintain a calm presence.
- **Use steady, calm movements**: Avoid sudden gestures or quick movements. These can escalate tension. Instead, use slow, deliberate motions to maintain a sense of control and calmness.

The way you physically position yourself can immediately lower the perceived threat level. People naturally mirror the emotions and energy they're surrounded by, so when you model calmness, you invite others to follow suit.

THE CLARA METHOD: A FRAMEWORK FOR QUICK DE-ESCALATION

Sometimes, you need a structured approach to bring the emotional intensity down, and that's where the **CLARA method** comes in. This is a simple, step-by-step approach you can use to engage with the person or situation without escalating emotions.

Here's how to use the CLARA method in a high-pressure moment:

- **Centre**: Take a moment to centre yourself. Breathe deeply, steady your emotions and focus on staying calm. Your inner state sets the tone for the conversation.
- **Learn**: Listen to what the other person is saying without interrupting. Often, people just need to feel heard and giving them space to express themselves can defuse much of the tension.
- **Articulate**: Once they've had a chance to speak, reflect back what you've heard. Say something like, "I hear that you're frustrated because..." This shows you're not just listening; you're understanding.
- **Receive**: Be open to their response. You may not agree, but receiving their perspective without judgment keeps the conversation constructive.
- **Accomplish**: Shift the conversation toward resolution. Ask, "How can we move forward from here?". This question redirects the energy from conflict to problem-solving.

By following this simple process, you're not only calming the situation but also building trust and showing that you're a leader who listens and values the input of others.

THE POWER OF LANGUAGE: FROM CONFLICT TO COLLABORATION

Words matter. In moments of conflict, what you say and how you say it can either escalate the situation or defuse it. When emotions are high, people tend to react impulsively, often making the situation worse. But with the right language, you can quickly change the tone of the conversation.

Try these phrases to shift from conflict to collaboration:

- **"I want to understand your perspective"**: This phrase shows empathy and a willingness to listen, which immediately reduces defensiveness.
- **"Let's find a solution together"**: Instead of focusing on the problem, this language shifts the focus to collaboration, making the other person feel like they're part of the solution.
- **"What would help in this situation?"**: By asking for their input, you're giving them a sense of control, which can calm emotions and lead to a more productive conversation.

One key element is **avoiding directive language** like "calm down" or "relax". These commands often have the opposite effect, increasing frustration. Instead, use language that invites understanding and collaboration.

TAKING A STEP BACK: THE POWER OF SPACE AND TIME

When things get intense, sometimes the best action is inaction. Taking a step back, literally or figuratively, can give everyone involved the breathing room they need to cool off.

How to use space and time effectively in a tense situation:

- **Take a physical step back**: If you're too close, step back a bit. This gives the person space, which can reduce feelings of being cornered or pressured.
- **Suggest a pause**: If things are getting heated, suggest a quick break. Say something like, "Let's take five minutes and come back to this". Often, a brief pause is all it takes to reset emotions and approach the problem with fresh eyes.

- **Create physical space**: If possible, move to a different environment. A change of setting can help shift the energy and bring down the intensity of the situation.

Giving space, both physically and mentally, shows that you're not rushing to push your agenda. It shows you're confident enough to allow things to cool off before continuing, which is a sign of strong leadership.

NON-VERBAL CUES: COMMUNICATING CALM WITHOUT SAYING A WORD

Non-verbal cues are incredibly powerful. In fact, studies show that much of our communication is non-verbal, meaning how you look and act can say more than what you actually say.

Key non-verbal cues to use when de-escalating a situation:

- **Eye Contact**: Maintaining soft, steady eye contact shows that you're present and engaged without coming across as aggressive. Don't stare, but make sure your eyes communicate calmness.
- **Facial Expressions**: Keep your facial expressions neutral or slightly concerned — anything too intense can fuel the fire.
- **Tone of Voice**: Your tone can either calm or inflame a situation. Keep your voice steady and low, avoiding sharp or high-pitched tones, which can sound confrontational.

Even when you're not speaking, your body language and expressions are constantly communicating. Being mindful of this helps you create a calming, reassuring presence, even when emotions are high.

THE SCIENCE BEHIND IT: HOW YOUR BRAIN RESPONDS TO THREATS

Why do these techniques work? It all comes down to how our brains react to perceived threats. When we feel threatened, whether physically or emotionally, our **amygdala** (the part of the brain responsible for fight-or-flight) kicks in. This makes us react impulsively, which can escalate the situation if we're not careful.

However, when you use calming body language, empathetic language and give space, you're signaling to the brain that there's no threat, which helps switch off the fight-or-flight response. This shifts people out of survival mode and into a state where they can think clearly and rationally again.

HOW TO PUT THIS INTO PRACTICE

Let's make this practical. Next time you find yourself in a tense situation, try this quick de-escalation approach:

1. **Pause and breathe**: Take a deep breath and check your body language. Are you tense? Relax your posture and maintain an open stance.
2. **Engage with empathy**: Use language that acknowledges the other person's emotions — "I can see you're feeling frustrated. Let's talk about it."
3. **Stay steady**: Keep your voice calm and avoid getting defensive. Model the calmness you want to see in the other person.
4. **Take a step back if needed**: Physically or verbally take a step back to give the situation space to breathe. "Let's take five and come back to this" can work wonders in high-pressure moments.

5. **Use non-verbal cues**: Maintain soft eye contact, keep your tone neutral and use relaxed gestures to lower the emotional intensity.

KEY TAKEAWAYS

- **Non-threatening body language**: Stay open, relaxed and calm to instantly lower the perceived threat level.
- **The CLARA method**: Use this simple framework to stay centred and guide conversations from tension to resolution.
- **Empathetic language**: Words matter. Use language that promotes understanding and collaboration, not confrontation.
- **Create space**: Physically or mentally step back to allow emotions to settle before continuing.
- **Non-verbal communication**: Sometimes, how you say something matters more than what you say. Be mindful of your tone, body language and eye contact.

By mastering these de-escalation techniques, you'll be able to stay in control, manage high-pressure situations with ease and maintain your authority — all while fostering an environment of respect and collaboration. It's not just about calming the storm; it's about navigating through it with confidence and grace.

CHAPTER TEN SUMMARY FOR THE ART OF SHIFTING QUICKLY

When challenges arise, the faster we can reset our nervous system and regain our cognitive clarity, the more capable we are of making strategic decisions and maintaining balance under pressure.

KEY INSIGHTS AND TECHNIQUES

1. Why Stress Disrupts Our Thinking

- Stress triggers the fight-or-flight response, redirecting energy away from our brain's logical and creative centres to prepare our bodies for physical action. This "amygdala hijack" results in impulsive, reactive decisions rather than thoughtful, strategic ones.

2. The Importance of Shifting Quickly

- The real test of leadership isn't about avoiding stress but about how swiftly we can recalibrate and return to clarity. Staying in a reactive state for too long can lead to poor decisions and unnecessary tension.

3. Brainwave Modulation: A Tool for Instant Focus or Relaxation

- Brainwave modulation, using binaural beats, allows us to tap into desired mental states (like calm or focus) by aligning our brainwaves to specific frequencies:
  - *Alpha waves: For relaxation and creativity.*
  - *Beta waves: For alertness and focus.*
  - *Gamma waves: For peak cognitive performance and clarity.*
- Listening to binaural beats with noise-cancelling headphones, paired with deep breathing, can create rapid mental shifts, whether to calm nerves before a meeting or boost focus during a demanding task.

4. Physical Cues for a Sensory Reset

- Simple sensory techniques can quickly interrupt spiralling stress, such as:
  - *Tactile grounding: Holding or pressing textured objects.*
  - *Temperature contrast: Alternating between hot and cold sensations (e.g., holding a cold glass and then a warm cup).*

5. Neurological Anchoring for Emotional Shifts

- Anchoring involves creating a physical trigger (e.g., pressing your thumb and forefinger together) that becomes associated with positive emotions. Over time, this physical cue can instantly shift you into a desired emotional state, such as confidence or calmness.

6. Somatic Intelligence: Listening to Your Body

- Paying attention to physical stress cues like tight shoulders or a racing heart allows you to respond early, preventing escalation. Techniques like somatic mapping and gentle movement can release built-up tension and restore balance.

7. Movement Practices for State Shifting

- Engaging in movement, even for a few minutes, can help reset your mental state. Practices like stretching, yoga, or taking a quick walk release physical tension and promote mental clarity.

8. De-escalation Techniques for High-Pressure Situations

- Leadership often requires managing not just your own state but also the energy of others. Key de-escalation strategies include:
    - *Non-threatening body language: Stay relaxed and open to reduce tension.*
    - *The CLARA method: A framework for calming interactions: Centre, Learn, Articulate, Receive, and Accomplish.*
    - *Empathetic language: Phrases like "I understand how you're feeling" or "Let's find a solution together" can turn conflict into collaboration.*
    - *Creating space: Suggesting a pause or stepping back physically to allow emotions to settle.*

SECTION FOUR

SUSTAIN THE DESIRED STATE

Once you've reached your desired state, the key challenge is sustaining it. This is where many people falter. They achieve success but quickly fall back into old habits or burnout. Sustaining your desired state means embedding the right habits, mindsets and systems into your daily life to ensure your success isn't fleeting. It's about creating a lifestyle that supports long-term growth and achievement, rather than constantly riding the highs and lows of short-term wins. Sustaining success is about consistency, balance and knowing how to maintain your momentum without burnout.

11

DEVELOPING SUSTAINABLE LEADERSHIP STRATEGIES

You've probably felt overcommitted before, spinning so many plates that you're just waiting for one to come crashing down. Maybe you've hit milestones that most people dream of, yet underneath it all, something feels off. Success, influence, impact — they're all within your grasp, but there's a part of you wondering, *"Can I keep this up without losing myself in the process?"*.

True leadership isn't just about scaling new heights. It's about maintaining your success in a way that doesn't sacrifice your health, relationships or sanity. If you've ever thought, *"There has to be a way to keep pushing forward without feeling drained"*, then this chapter is for you.

In this chapter, we'll explore sustainable strategies that help you not just achieve success but *thrive* in all areas of your life. Real, long-lasting success doesn't come from running yourself into the ground. It comes from creating a balance that keeps your personal and professional life moving forward in harmony.

CREATING A PERSONAL SUSTAINABILITY PLAN

You wouldn't expect a business to thrive without a solid plan to manage its resources, so, why do we expect ourselves to keep going without one? Just like businesses create sustainability frameworks to ensure long-term growth, you need a **personal sustainability plan** – a strategy for balancing your work and life that maintains both your health and your success.

Think of it this way: your energy, focus and relationships are all resources. To keep everything running smoothly, you need to manage these resources as carefully as you would a budget.

DEFINING SUSTAINABILITY IN LEADERSHIP

To create a personal sustainability plan, you first need to ask yourself some key questions:

- Which parts of my life are most important but often get sacrificed for work?
- What activities help me recharge mentally and physically?
- How do I measure success beyond just hitting financial targets or career milestones?

This isn't about doing it all. It's about figuring out what truly matters and making sure those areas get the attention they deserve.

INCORPORATING STRATEGIC CHECK-INS

You've probably experienced that creeping sense of burnout – you hit a big goal but, instead of feeling on top of the world, you feel drained. That's because success without balance is a short-term win.

Just like businesses need regular performance reviews, leaders need regular self-reviews. But instead of just measuring professional success, these check-ins should focus on your well-being and relationships, too.

Here's how you can check in with yourself:

- **Weekly Energy Audits**: How's your energy? Are you running on fumes? Track your stress levels, physical energy and mental clarity. If you're running low, it's time to adjust before you hit a wall.
- **Monthly Relationship Assessments**: Have you been showing up for the people who matter most to you? Leadership can be lonely if you let work pull you away from personal connections. Relationships keep you grounded. Make sure you're not losing touch.
- **Quarterly Strategic Realignment**: Are your goals still aligned with where you want to go? It's easy to get caught up in the day-to-day grind but it's important to make sure your efforts are still leading you toward your long-term vision.

Get Help When You Need It: The reality is, you don't always have to go at it alone. At *The Achievement Algorithm*, we offer monthly 1-2-1 retainer packages which our clients tap into when they need a reset. Whether you need a quick tune-up, a mindset shift or just someone to check your blind spots, having that extra support on retainer can be a game-changer.

PRIORITISING STRATEGIC RELATIONSHIPS

Sustaining success isn't just about managing tasks, it's about managing relationships, too. But let's be real: you can't give *everyone* your full attention. The key is to focus on the relationships that truly matter — the ones that nourish you and help you grow.

Here's how to do it:

- **Dedicated Time for Close Relationships**: You can't run on an empty tank and personal connections refuel you. Carve out time for your family and friends — no distractions, no multitasking. Just be present.
- **Curate Your Professional Network**: Think of your mentors, peers and allies as your safety net. These are the people who will support you during high-pressure periods, offer advice and keep you grounded.
- **Set Relationship Goals**: Just like you set business goals, set goals for your relationships. Make sure you're nurturing the connections that matter most, both personally and professionally.

THE POWER OF SAYING NO

Here's the thing no one told you: **you don't have to do shit you don't want to.** Saying no isn't a sign of weakness, it's actually one of the most powerful tools in your leadership toolkit. Every time you say yes to something unimportant, you're actually saying no to something that might really matter.

It's easy to feel like saying yes to every opportunity is the way to succeed but let me tell you, it's the quickest path to burnout. The key is learning to say no strategically so that you're preserving your time and energy for the things that truly matter.

REFRAMING THE FEAR OF NO

We've all been there: someone asks you to do something and your gut says no, but out of obligation, you say yes anyway. Every yes to something unimportant is an implicit no to something meaningful. Success isn't about saying yes to everything, it's about knowing when to say no so you can focus on what's going to move the needle.

Saying no doesn't diminish your leadership. It demonstrates clarity of purpose, self-respect and strategic thinking. A leader who knows when and how to say no gains respect, not just for their decisiveness but for their ability to protect their most valuable asset: their focus.

MANAGING COGNITIVE OVERLOAD WITH MICRO-BREAKS

Even with strong boundaries, leadership can be mentally exhausting. That's where **micro-breaks** come in. These aren't long vacations or even hour-long breaks; they're small, intentional pauses throughout your day to reset your brain and prevent burnout.

How to Implement Micro-Breaks:

- **Step Away**: When you feel your focus slipping, take a five-minute walk or stretch. These tiny breaks recharge your mental energy and boost creativity.

- **Practice Mindfulness**: Even a sixty-second breathing exercise can make a difference. Close your eyes, focus on your breath and reset.
- **Disconnect Daily**: Take time to unplug from work, even if it's just for ten minutes. Whether it's stepping outside or listening to music, these brief moments of disconnection clear your mind.

PRACTISING MINIMALISM IN LEADERSHIP

As leaders, people like us are constantly pulled in multiple directions. The daily grind of meetings, emails and problem-solving can easily become overwhelming. We live in a world that glorifies busyness; often mistaking being "busy" for being productive. But what if the real power lay in doing less, not more?

The concept of minimalism in leadership, rooted in the Pareto Principle (the 80/20 rule), invites us to rethink how we spend our time and energy. The 80/20 rule tells us that 80% of results come from just 20% of our actions. In other words, a small portion of what we do delivers the majority of our success. The challenge for people like us is to figure out what that 20% really is and to focus on it relentlessly, letting go of the rest.

This isn't just theory; it's a game-changing approach that has been embraced by some of the world's most successful leaders. By practising minimalism, you'll free up time and mental space for high-impact work, preventing burnout and ensuring that your energy is invested where it truly matters.

THE 80/20 RULE IN LEADERSHIP: WORKING SMARTER, NOT HARDER

For people like us, the pressure to constantly do more can feel overwhelming. But think about it. How often do we find ourselves working long hours, only to feel like we're barely making a dent in what truly matters? The 80/20 rule gives us permission to step back, assess and refocus.

The 80/20 rule suggests that a small portion of your efforts will generate the majority of your outcomes. For us, this means letting go of the idea that we have to juggle every little task ourselves. Instead, we shift our focus to the few things that truly drive progress – the key decisions, strategic thinking and high-leverage actions that make a real difference.

Look at Warren Buffett, for example. He's mastered the art of focusing on what matters most. Buffett doesn't waste time on every investment opportunity that crosses his desk. Instead, he zeroes in on a few, high-impact decisions that generate 80% (or more) of his results. His disciplined focus on the most valuable opportunities is a big part of why he's one of the wealthiest and most respected investors in the world. It's a lesson for all of us: success isn't about doing everything; it's about doing the right things.

REAL-WORLD EXAMPLE: STEVE JOBS AND APPLE

When Steve Jobs returned to Apple in 1997, the company was on the brink of collapse. One of his first moves was to drastically simplify Apple's product line. At the time, Apple was producing dozens of products, spreading itself too thin and losing focus. Jobs slashed the product range down to just four key products – a desktop, a laptop and consumer and professional versions of each.

By focusing the company's resources on a few high-impact areas, Jobs positioned Apple to become more innovative and successful. This laser focus led to the creation of the iMac, iPod, iPhone and iPad — products that revolutionised industries and drove Apple's growth into the world's most valuable company.

The lesson here? People like us need to focus on fewer, more impactful tasks. When we spread ourselves too thin, we dilute our effectiveness. But when we cut through the noise and zero in on what truly matters, we're able to make far greater strides.

HOW TO IDENTIFY THE 20% THAT MATTERS

So, how do we, as leaders, figure out what the critical 20% of activities are? It requires stepping back and evaluating our tasks and responsibilities from a high-level perspective. Here's how you can start identifying where to focus your energy:

1. **Evaluate Your Tasks by Impact**: Begin by listing all the tasks you typically handle in a week. Now, look at them through the lens of impact. Which tasks directly move you closer to your goals? Which ones are merely maintaining the status quo? Prioritise the ones that make a difference and either delegate or drop the rest.
2. **Look at Past Results**: Reflect on the last year or quarter. Which projects or decisions had the biggest impact on your success? Which ones took up a lot of time but didn't move the needle? History leaves clues. If you look carefully, you'll start to see patterns that help you focus your efforts moving forward.

3. **Delegate Low-Value Tasks**: Once you've identified your high-impact tasks, it's time to clear your plate of the lower-value work. Trust your team with responsibilities that don't require your unique input and free yourself up for the deep, strategic work that only you can do.
4. **Set Clear Metrics for Success**: Success is easier to chase when it's measurable. What are the key metrics or outcomes that matter most to you and your organisation? If a task doesn't align with these outcomes, it's likely not part of the 20%. Stay focused on what drives those key results.
5. **Create Time for Deep Work**: Once you know what your critical tasks are, block out dedicated time to work on them. This is your "deep work" time, free from distractions, where you can focus on strategy, vision and innovation — the kind of work that drives your success.

By taking these steps, you'll start to see that focusing on the 20% of high-impact tasks not only simplifies your workload but also amplifies your results.

GREGG MCKEOWN'S ESSENTIALISM: THE DISCIPLINED PURSUIT OF LESS

Greg McKeown's book, *Essentialism: The Disciplined Pursuit of Less,* takes this concept of minimalism one step further. It's not just about doing less, but about doing *only* what is essential. For people like us, this means saying no to good opportunities in order to focus on the great ones.

McKeown argues that many of us are stretched too thin because we fail to distinguish between what is truly essential and what is merely good or desirable. The essentialist mindset pushes us to ruthlessly prioritise and cut out the clutter in our lives, so we can focus on what matters most. This discipline is what helps leaders avoid burnout and perform at their best over the long term.

Take Jeff Weiner, CEO of LinkedIn, as an example. Weiner deliberately schedules time for "thinking" each day. Despite the demands of leading a fast-growing tech company, he knows that his greatest contributions come from deep, strategic thinking, not from managing a million small tasks. By embracing essentialism, he creates space in his schedule for the kind of work that moves the business forward in a meaningful way.

How We Can Practise Essentialism

- **Prioritise Ruthlessly**: It's not enough to do less; we need to do *less but better*. This requires tough decisions and the willingness to say no to non-essential tasks.
- **Protect Your Time**: Carve out time for the most important work — the things that drive real value and progress. Guard this time fiercely.
- **Say No With Confidence**: Learning to say no is crucial. We're often conditioned to say yes to everything, but saying no frees up time and energy for the tasks that align with our long-term vision.

By adopting essentialism, we stop trying to do it all. Instead, we focus on what truly drives success, leaving behind the distractions that can drain our time and energy.

LINKING TO THE ONE THING PRINCIPLE

The ideas of minimalism and essentialism are closely aligned with the principle of *The One Thing,* as outlined in Gary Keller and Jay Papasan's book. The core message is simple: extraordinary success comes from focusing on *the single most important task* — the one thing that, if done, makes everything else easier or unnecessary.

For leaders like us, this means figuring out what that "one thing" is at any given moment. Keller's approach builds on the 80/20 rule by narrowing our focus even further. Instead of spreading ourselves thin across multiple priorities, we zoom in on the one task or goal that will make the greatest impact.

Bill Gates is a great example of someone who practised this principle. In the early days of Microsoft, Gates focused almost exclusively on writing and perfecting software. He didn't try to do everything at once. His one thing was ensuring that Microsoft's software dominated the market. By staying laser-focused on this single priority, Gates built Microsoft into the behemoth it is today.

How to Practise The One Thing in Your Leadership

1. **Ask the Right Question**: Start by asking yourself, "What's the one thing I can do such that by doing it, everything else will be easier or unnecessary?" This question cuts through the noise and helps you zero in on the task that will drive the greatest progress.
2. **Focus Relentlessly**: Once you've identified your one thing, commit to it. Block out distractions and delegate lower-priority tasks. Protect your time and focus like your success depends on it — because it does.

3. **Track Progress**: Regularly assess whether your efforts are moving the needle on your one thing. If not, adjust your strategy or refocus your time to ensure you're making meaningful progress.

By adopting *The One Thing* principle, you align your energy with what truly matters. You'll find that this focused approach leads to greater efficiency, less stress and more impactful results.

PUTTING IT ALL TOGETHER: MINIMALISM, ESSENTIALISM AND THE ONE THING

For leaders like us, the challenge isn't doing more, it's doing more of the right things. Practising minimalism, embracing essentialism and focusing on *The One Thing* allows us to cut through the distractions, focus on what truly drives success and lead with more clarity and impact.

By stripping away the unnecessary and honing in on the essential, we can lead more effectively, prevent burnout and build a sustainable path to long-term success, both personally and professionally. This isn't just about working smarter, it's about living smarter, too.

As you move forward, remember: the real power lies in simplicity. The more we focus on the few things that truly matter, the more extraordinary our results will be.

CHAPTER 11 SUMMARY FOR DEVELOPING SUSTAINABLE LEADERSHIP STRATEGIES

1. The Need for a Personal Sustainability Plan

Just as businesses need frameworks to ensure growth, leaders need personal sustainability plans. This means managing your energy, focus, and relationships as carefully as any other resource. By prioritising what truly matters, you can ensure you're progressing in both your personal and professional life without burnout.

Key Questions to Define Your Plan:

- What parts of my life are most important but often sacrificed for work?
- What activities help me recharge physically and mentally?
- How do I define success beyond financial or professional milestones?

2. Regular Strategic Check-ins

Success without balance is short-lived. Regular self-reviews can prevent burnout and ensure alignment with long-term goals.

- **Weekly Energy Audits**: Assess stress levels, physical energy, and mental clarity.
- **Monthly Relationship Assessments**: Check if you're prioritising time for the people who matter.

- **Quarterly Strategic Realignment**: Revisit your goals to ensure they still align with your vision.

Support Tip: Retainer packages like those offered by The Achievement Algorithm can provide the external accountability and mindset shifts you need when life gets off track.

3. Prioritising Strategic Relationships

Sustained success is built on meaningful relationships. Leaders need to focus on connections that nourish and support growth.

- **Dedicate Time to Close Relationships**: Be present with family and friends.
- **Curate Your Professional Network**: Lean on mentors, peers, and allies who help you grow.
- **Set Relationship Goals**: Just like professional goals, ensure you're nurturing connections that matter.

4. The Power of Saying No

Every time you say yes to something unimportant, you say no to something that truly matters. Saying no strategically is a powerful tool for preserving time and energy for high-impact work.

- Reframe the fear of no: Saying no demonstrates clarity, self-respect, and focus.
- Protect your priorities by confidently declining tasks or opportunities that don't align with your goals.

5. Managing Cognitive Overload With Micro-Breaks

Leadership can be mentally exhausting. Micro-breaks are short, intentional pauses to recharge and prevent burnout.

- **Step Away**: Take a five-minute walk or stretch when focus slips.
- **Practice Mindfulness**: A 60-second breathing exercise can reset your mind.
- **Disconnect Daily**: Spend 10 minutes unplugged to clear your thoughts.

6. Practising Minimalism in Leadership

Success isn't about doing more; it's about focusing on less but better. The **Pareto Principle (80/20 rule)** reminds us that 80% of results come from 20% of actions. Identify and prioritise high-impact tasks, then delegate or eliminate the rest.

- Look at leaders like Steve Jobs, who simplified Apple's product line to focus on innovation, or Warren Buffett, who concentrates on a few key investments. Their success stems from disciplined focus on what truly matters.

7. Essentialism: The Disciplined Pursuit of Less

Inspired by Greg McKeown's *Essentialism,* this approach pushes leaders to prioritise only what is essential, cutting out non-essential tasks and distractions.

- **Prioritise Ruthlessly**: Focus only on what drives the most value.
- **Protect Your Time**: Block time for critical work and guard it fiercely.
- **Say No With Confidence**: Decline opportunities that don't align with your core priorities.

8. The One Thing Principle

Gary Keller's *The One Thing* urges leaders to focus on the single task or goal that makes everything else easier or unnecessary.

- **Ask the Right Question**: "What's the one thing I can do that will make the greatest impact?"
- **Focus Relentlessly**: Once identified, commit to that one thing and eliminate distractions.
- **Track Progress**: Regularly assess if your efforts are driving results.

12

THE REST IS WORK

In the relentless push to meet goals, it's easy to forget one essential truth: rest is not the enemy of success, it's the fuel. Most of us have this backwards. We think that grinding nonstop will get us ahead, but constantly pushing yourself without taking intentional breaks is a fast track to burnout and diminishing returns. It's not just about surviving today's workload; it's about sustaining yourself for the long game.

Here's the real insight: **rest fuels success.** It doesn't take away from it. The moments when you step away from your work, take a breather or even completely unplug are the times when your mind has the space to reset, refocus and tap into creative energy that wasn't accessible before. You're not being "lazy" or "unproductive" during these moments – you're giving your brain the time it needs to refuel and come back sharper.

WHY REST FUELS CREATIVITY AND SUCCESS

Think about it. When you're grinding through task after task, what happens? You get tunnel vision. Your brain is so focused on the immediate demands that it doesn't have the bandwidth for creative thinking or problem-solving. But when you step away, whether it's a ten-minute walk, a short meditation, or even a full day off, you give your brain the space to breathe.

Rest unlocks creativity because your mind stops being weighed down by the noise of to-do lists and deadlines. It's during these breaks that your subconscious mind can work through problems, make new connections and come up with solutions that weren't obvious when you were in the thick of it. You've probably had those "aha!" moments in the shower or while driving, right? That's no coincidence. Your brain does its best thinking when it's given a little space.

THE POWER OF STRATEGIC REST

Strategic rest is about more than just getting enough sleep or taking a break when you're exhausted. It's about **intentionally building downtime into your routine** — not waiting until you're burned out, but regularly scheduling those moments to recharge before you hit a wall. Just like athletes train hard but build in recovery days to allow their bodies to repair and strengthen, leaders need to do the same for their minds and creativity.

By deliberately incorporating rest, you'll find that you actually **increase your capacity for high-level performance.** When you pause, you're not losing momentum, you're preparing yourself to move forward with more clarity, focus and creativity.

SHIFTING YOUR MINDSET ON REST

We live in a culture that glorifies busyness. Many of us wear exhaustion as a badge of honour, thinking that being constantly "on" means we're productive. But here's the thing: being busy doesn't equal being effective. Rest is not a weakness; it's a strategy. The most successful people know when to push and when to pull back.

Let's shift the narrative: **rest is work**. It's the part of your process that ensures you can continue to lead, innovate and grow over the long term. Without it, you're just running on fumes and that's when mistakes happen, creativity dries up and the joy of what you do fades.

REST AS A COMPETITIVE ADVANTAGE

Think about this: when you're well-rested and recharged, your ability to **make better decisions** improves. You have more mental clarity, you're less reactive and you're able to see the big picture. You're not just putting out fires — you're thinking strategically, setting the vision and leading with purpose. Rest allows you to stay a step ahead, not just get through the day.

Leaders who don't embrace rest end up drained, which leads to diminished problem-solving skills and decreased creativity. They become more prone to stress, emotional reactivity and decision fatigue. Meanwhile, leaders who understand the value of rest are more resilient, innovative and, ultimately, more successful.

ACTIONABLE STEPS TO INCORPORATE REST INTO YOUR ROUTINE

1. **Schedule Breaks Like Meetings**: Block out time in your calendar for short breaks throughout the day. Don't leave it to chance — make rest part of your daily routine, not something that happens only when you're exhausted.
2. **Embrace Micro-Breaks**: Even a five-minute pause between tasks can make a world of difference. Use this time to step away from your desk, stretch or take a quick walk to reset your mind and energy.
3. **Create Digital Detox Times**: Spend time away from screens, especially after long stretches of work. Give your eyes and brain a break from constant stimulation.
4. **Engage in Activities That Recharge You**: Whether it's meditation, exercise, reading, or spending time in nature, find the activities that help you unwind and schedule them regularly. These aren't luxuries, they're essential to keeping you at your best.
5. **Build in Longer Breaks**: Plan for days or weekends off to fully disconnect. Whether it's a weekend getaway or simply turning off your phone for a day, give yourself the space to reset fully.

THE BOTTOM LINE

The rest isn't just something we do when there's time — it's what gives us the energy to **keep creating, innovating and leading**. If you want to sustain your success and reach new heights, it starts with understanding that rest is part of the equation. It's time to stop viewing breaks as the enemy of productivity and start seeing them as the secret weapon that fuels your success.

So, next time you feel that pull to keep going when you're running on empty, remember: the most productive thing you can do might just be stepping away. **The rest is the work** that powers everything else.

WORKING SMARTER, NOT HARDER: THE CHALLENGE OF ATTENTION RESIDUE

You've probably been there — you wrap up one task, but your mind is still stuck on it even as you dive into the next. It's like carrying baggage from one meeting into the next. That lingering mental focus is what Sophie Leroy, in her 2009 study, called **attention residue**. Simply put, part of your mental energy is still tangled up in the previous task, leaving you distracted and less effective at tackling what's in front of you.

When this happens, your ability to focus fully and think strategically takes a hit. You might be physically present in the room or on the next Zoom call, but mentally? You're still stuck on that last email or unresolved conversation. Leroy's research found that when we don't fully disengage from one task before starting another, our performance suffers — especially on tasks requiring problem-solving or high-level thinking. It's not just about how busy we are; it's about how *well* we switch gears.

What you really need are **longer, more intentional breaks** to clear out that mental clutter. These breaks allow your brain to reset so that when you dive into the next challenge, you're focused, fresh and not dragging along thoughts from the previous task. This is where working smarter, not harder, comes into play.

Sound familiar? You're not alone.

In 2011, a study by Alejandro Lleras and his team from the University of Illinois dug deeper into how breaks affect focus. Participants were asked to complete a fifty-minute task requiring sustained attention. Half worked straight through, while the other half took brief, intentional breaks. The results were eye-opening. Those who took breaks performed significantly better. The group that didn't take breaks saw their performance decline, while the break-takers stayed sharp, productive and engaged.

Lleras' conclusion? Even a **brief pause** can help your brain reset and improve cognitive function when you return to work. That's a game-changer for leaders and high-performers like us. It's proof that taking breaks isn't a luxury, it's a **performance strategy**.

This research highlights something crucial: when we step away from a task, our brain undergoes a process called **deactivation** — a moment where we let go of the mental baggage. Then, when we return to the task, we experience **reactivation**, where our brain comes back stronger, refreshed and ready to take on the next challenge with clarity and energy. By momentarily disengaging, you actually boost your capacity for **problem-solving and creative thinking**.

So, the next time you feel tempted to push through without a break, remember this: stepping back might be exactly what you need to come back sharper, more focused and ready to perform at your best. **Working smarter** means giving yourself those moments to reset, so you're not just grinding through the day, you're thriving in it.

THE SCIENCE BEHIND MICRO-BREAKS

Let's face it, pushing through the day without breaks might feel productive, but it's far from efficient. In reality, taking regular **micro-breaks** is one of the smartest ways to keep your energy levels consistent and prevent burnout. The science backs it up.

Our brains have a **finite capacity for sustained focus**. The more mental resources you drain, the more performance starts to slip — especially on tasks that require problem-solving, strategic thinking or creativity. But here's where **micro-breaks** work their magic. These brief pauses allow your brain to reset, replenishing your mental reserves so you can come back sharper and more focused.

It's all tied to something called **ultradian rhythms**, your body's natural productivity cycle. Think of this like your internal work clock. It runs in 90- to 120-minute bursts of energy, after which, your body signals that it needs a break. It's your brain's way of saying, "Time to step back for a moment". These rhythms regulate everything from hormone release to brain activity, telling you when to push hard and when to ease off.

When you respect this cycle, you maximise your focus during the **high-energy phase** — the part of the cycle where you're in the zone, crushing those key tasks, making big decisions or solving complex problems. But after about ninety minutes, your energy drops, and that's when it's time for a **micro-break**. If you ignore this natural dip and push through, your focus weakens, mental fatigue sets in and the quality of your decisions takes a hit.

For leaders, this is especially critical. We've all felt the effects of **decision fatigue** when the brain gets overloaded and simple choices suddenly feel like a struggle. By taking well-timed breaks, you can keep your brain fresh, preventing that overload before it leads to mistakes or poor judgement.

What's more, respecting these cycles does wonders for **emotional regulation,** a key factor in leadership. When you're mentally fatigued, emotions run high. You're more likely to be reactive, stressed or frustrated. By stepping back for short, restorative pauses, you can reset emotionally, making it easier to stay calm and composed under pressure. And let's be honest, a leader who can keep their cool when things heat up is worth their weight in gold.

PRACTICAL APPLICATION OF ULTRADIAN RHYTHMS FOR LEADERS

So how do you actually apply this in your day-to-day leadership role? It's all about **working with** your body's natural rhythms, not against them.

1. **Work in ninety-minute intervals**: Break your day into focused ninety-minute sprints, followed by a ten- to fifteen-minute break. Use that high-energy phase for the big, important tasks.
2. **Use breaks strategically**: Avoid mentally draining activities during your break. Instead, opt for something restorative, like stretching, walking or even a quick meditation. It's about letting your brain switch off for a bit.
3. **Schedule critical tasks during peak cycles**: Pay attention to when your body naturally feels more alert and schedule high-priority tasks during those times. You'll notice a big difference in your productivity.

4. **Listen to your body**: When you feel tired or lose focus, don't push through it. That's your brain telling you it's time to rest. Ignoring these signals leads to mental fatigue and reduced effectiveness.

Not all tasks are created equal, and the length of your break should reflect that. A 2023 study by the British Psychological Society found that **micro-breaks** work wonders for routine tasks by keeping mind-wandering in check and minimising mistakes. But when it comes to creative or complex tasks, longer breaks (ten to fifteen minutes) provide a much-needed mental reset. This means you can tailor your break times depending on the nature of the work you're doing — shorter breaks for repetitive tasks and longer pauses for strategic thinking or problem-solving sessions.

HOW TO PERSONALISE YOUR MICRO-BREAKS

Here's the beauty of it: there's no one-size-fits-all when it comes to taking breaks. You need to find what works best for you.

- **For physical energy boosts**: Set a timer to stand up, stretch or walk around every hour. Even a small change in your posture or environment can refresh your focus.
- **For mental clarity**: If you need to reset mentally, try a mindfulness-based break. Focus on your breathing or simply observe your surroundings. After a big meeting, take a minute to mentally "reset" before moving on to the next task.
- **For emotional recovery**: Engage in something that lifts your mood, whether it's listening to music, journaling or stepping outside for fresh air. Sometimes, a quick moment to yourself can make all the difference.

INTEGRATING NATURE INTO BREAKS

Never underestimate the power of nature. Even if you can't step outside, bring the outdoors in by adding plants or natural elements to your workspace. If you have time, take **micro-walks** outside to clear your head and get some fresh perspective.

DIGITAL DETOX BREAKS

Lastly, for those of us glued to screens all day, consider a **digital detox**. Step away from the phone, the computer and the notifications for just a few minutes. Let your brain rest from the constant stimulation.

- **No-Screen Zones**: Create screen-free times in your day, like during lunch or short breaks. It gives your eyes a rest and your mind a chance to disconnect.
- **Mindful Detachment**: When you take a break, really step away. Don't check your phone or emails; just engage with the moment and let your mind wander.

By embracing these rhythms and integrating micro-breaks into your day, you'll find that you're not only more productive, but you're also more creative, focused and better equipped to handle whatever comes your way. **The rest is just as important as the work**, so give yourself the breaks you deserve.

CHAPTER TWELVE CHECKLIST FOR THE REST IS WORK

In this chapter, we dismantled the myth that rest is a luxury or a sign of laziness. Instead, we explored how rest is a critical element of sustainable success. Far from being an interruption to productivity, rest is the fuel that powers creativity, clarity, and long-term achievement. This chapter provided actionable strategies to integrate rest into your routine, helping you lead smarter, not harder.

KEY TAKEAWAYS

1. Rest as a Performance Strategy

- Rest is not the enemy of success; it's the foundation of it. When we rest, we allow our minds to reset, refocus, and access creative problem-solving abilities that are inaccessible during periods of constant work.
- Strategic rest ensures you can sustain high performance over the long term, avoiding burnout and diminished returns.

2. The Science Behind Rest and Creativity

- Rest unlocks creativity by giving the brain space to process, connect ideas, and find innovative solutions.
- Moments of rest — like a walk or a break from screens — often lead to "aha!" moments as your subconscious mind works through problems.

3. Shifting the Narrative: Rest Is Work

- Society glorifies busyness, but busyness does not equal effectiveness. Rest is a powerful tool that ensures better decision-making, problem-solving, and strategic thinking.
- Reframing rest as part of your workflow, rather than something "extra", helps you maintain balance and creativity.

4. Combatting Attention Residue

- Attention residue occurs when your focus lingers on a previous task, making it harder to fully engage with the next.
- To combat this, intentional breaks allow your brain to disengage from one task and reset for the next, improving performance and focus.

ACTIONABLE STRATEGIES FOR INCORPORATING REST

1. Schedule Breaks Like Meetings

- Block regular, intentional breaks into your day. Make rest as non-negotiable as your most important meetings.

2. Embrace Micro-Breaks

- Short pauses, even as brief as five minutes, can help clear mental clutter and refresh your focus.
- Use this time to stretch, walk, or engage in mindfulness.

3. Utilise Ultradian Rhythms

- Work in 90-minute cycles followed by 10–15 minute breaks, aligning with your body's natural productivity rhythms.
- Respecting these cycles helps prevent fatigue, improve focus, and enhance emotional regulation.

4. Incorporate Nature

- Engage with nature during breaks, even if it's a short walk outside or adding plants to your workspace. Nature enhances mental clarity and reduces stress.

5. Digital Detox

- Step away from screens during breaks to reduce mental overstimulation.
- Create screen-free zones in your day to allow your brain to truly relax.

6. Build in Longer Breaks

- Plan for days off or extended breaks to fully reset. Whether it's a weekend away or simply unplugging from work for a day, longer pauses are essential for sustained performance.

SECTION FIVE

EXPAND BEYOND YOUR LIMITS

This is where the magic happens. This is when you realise that your potential for success goes far beyond what you thought possible. When you've aligned your actions, increased your capacity and learned how to sustain success, you're primed to push beyond your limits. Expansion is about growth, stepping into new realms of potential and opening up to opportunities that once felt out of reach. True breakthroughs happen here, where you discover that your capacity for success is far greater than you ever imagined.

13

EXPANDING YOUR CAPACITY FOR SUCCESS

You've probably heard the phrase "working smarter, not harder", but what if your biggest wins didn't come from making small, incremental improvements but from **quantum leaps**? Picture this: instead of inching forward, step by step, what if you could make a sudden, dramatic leap in your results? That's the magic of expanding your capacity for success. It's not about doing more; it's about **becoming** more. It's about evolving into someone who can thrive at an entirely new level.

Quantum leaps are those game-changing moments where progress happens in an instant, completely defying conventional wisdom. These breakthroughs aren't just for Silicon Valley startups, they're possible for anyone willing to shift their mindset and take bold, unconventional steps. This chapter will help you crack the code to sustainable success by aligning your energy, shifting your mindset and evolving into the person capable of handling success at a whole new level.

QUANTUM LEAPS IN SUCCESS: MOVING BEYOND INCREMENTAL PROGRESS

We've been taught to believe that success comes from slow, steady progress. But what if the biggest breakthroughs come from making a **sudden, exponential leap** — like flipping a switch? A quantum leap is a complete paradigm shift, where you experience a sudden, almost out-of-nowhere jump to a higher level of performance or success.

Consider **Netflix**, which transformed from a DVD rental service into a streaming giant seemingly overnight. Or **Tesla**, which went from a niche electric car maker to revolutionising the entire automotive industry. These aren't small steps forward — they're **quantum leaps**. The common thread? Leaders at these companies didn't just tweak their strategies; they reimagined what was possible, took bold action and disrupted themselves before the market could do it for them.

CRACKING THE CODE TO QUANTUM LEAPS

What's the secret to making these giant leaps? It's about rethinking the way we approach success. Quantum leaps require a shift in mindset. It's not about working longer hours or grinding harder; it's about aligning your thoughts, energy and actions with a new way of thinking.

Quantum physics teaches us that particles don't move smoothly from one point to another, they "jump." They leap from one state to another without passing through the space in between. It's a perfect metaphor for how success can work.

You don't have to follow the conventional path, step by step. Sometimes, the biggest jumps come from thinking differently, acting boldly and stepping outside the lines of what you've been taught.

Quantum leaps in success are possible when we stop viewing progress as linear and start embracing the potential for **nonlinear growth**. When you open yourself to the idea that massive breakthroughs can happen, you begin to see opportunities where others see limitations.

THE POWER OF DISRUPTIVE UNLEARNING

To achieve a quantum leap, you often need to **unlearn** old habits and assumptions that got you where you are but won't take you where you want to go next. This is called **disruptive unlearning**. It's the willingness to let go of methods, beliefs or systems that may have worked in the past but are now holding you back.

Consider **Amazon**, which started as an online bookstore. Jeff Bezos and his team didn't just focus on becoming the best bookstore, they reimagined their entire business, unlearning the idea that they were just in the book business. This mindset shift paved the way for Amazon to become a powerhouse in everything from cloud computing to groceries.

Unlearning is uncomfortable because it forces you to challenge your own success. But this is exactly what opens the door to explosive growth. Ask yourself: *What beliefs am I holding onto that might be limiting my future?* Leaders who excel at disruptive unlearning make space for new opportunities and innovative ways of thinking that drive their next quantum leap forward.

LEVERAGING SERENDIPITY FOR QUANTUM LEAPS

Sometimes, quantum leaps don't come from perfectly executed plans. They happen through **serendipity** – those unexpected moments where chance encounters or random ideas lead to breakthrough opportunities. But here's the thing: successful leaders don't leave success to luck. They create environments where serendipity is more likely to happen.

Steve Jobs understood this well when he said, "You can't connect the dots looking forward; you can only connect them looking backwards". Jobs knew that being in the right place at the right time wasn't just about luck – it was about creating opportunities for collaboration, innovation and new ideas.

Christian Busch, author of *The Serendipity Mindset*, calls this **engineering serendipity**. Leaders who excel at leveraging serendipity deliberately create opportunities for chance encounters that can spark new ideas. They build diverse networks, attend events outside their usual industry and stay open to unexpected perspectives. When you intentionally seek out environments where random events can collide, you increase the likelihood of discovering new, game-changing opportunities.

For example, **Google's 20% time policy,** where employees could spend 20% of their work time on side projects, led to the creation of Gmail and AdSense. These innovations weren't planned, but they came about because the company gave space for unexpected ideas to flourish. Leaders who engineer serendipity understand that some of the best opportunities come from stepping outside their comfort zone.

CONNECTING THE DOTS: TURNING SERENDIPITY INTO STRATEGY

It's one thing to stumble across a great idea, but the real magic happens when you learn to **connect the dots**, turning random moments into actionable breakthroughs. Leaders who succeed at this have the ability to see patterns and link seemingly unrelated ideas together to form innovative strategies.

Elon Musk is a perfect example of this. He saw the connection between his interests in space exploration, renewable energy and electric cars and turned those separate ventures into a unified mission to revolutionise the future of humanity. It wasn't just luck that **SpaceX**, **Tesla** and **SolarCity** all came together, it was Musk's ability to see the larger picture and connect the dots in ways others couldn't.

In quantum mechanics, **superposition** refers to a particle's ability to exist in multiple states at once until it is observed. Leaders must embrace this concept, holding multiple possibilities in their minds, embracing uncertainty and allowing creativity to flourish. When you connect the dots in unexpected ways, you open the door to game-changing insights and quantum leaps.

THE NECESSARY STEPS BEFORE THE QUANTUM LEAP

Quantum leaps don't just happen out of nowhere. They require a foundation. You've probably heard stories of overnight successes but what's often left out is the **work, learning and mindset shifts** that led up to that breakthrough moment.

In this book, we've worked through key steps that are essential to reaching the stage where a quantum leap becomes possible. The journey we've taken through earlier chapters isn't just prep work, it's the necessary groundwork for understanding and **executing the leap** when the time is right.

Why is that? Because quantum leaps require more than just ambition or a burst of energy. They demand **clarity, readiness and a deep understanding** of where you are and where you're going. You have to know what's no longer serving you, be open to new perspectives and have the mental capacity to see opportunities when they arise. It's not about jumping blindly, it's about making a calculated, informed leap to the next level.

Consider elite athletes. They train for years to build the muscle memory, strength, and focus that allows them to execute incredible feats in moments that matter. The leap itself looks fast, but the preparation is painstaking. Likewise, every step we've taken in this journey has been about strengthening your foundation — mentally, emotionally, and strategically — so that when the opportunity for a quantum leap arrives, you're not only ready for it, but capable of sustaining the new level of success it brings.

QUANTUM LEAPS AND SUSTAINABLE LEADERSHIP

The real beauty of quantum leaps is that they don't just lead to one big win — they set you up for **sustainable success** over the long term. It's not enough to make a breakthrough once. You need to have the capacity, systems and resilience to maintain and grow from that success.

Consider **Netflix** again. After launching its streaming platform, Netflix didn't sit back and relax. The company continually evolved, investing in original content and adapting its business model to stay ahead of the competition. Quantum leaps aren't just about one-off wins — they're about expanding your capacity to **handle success and keep growing**.

So, how do you build that capacity for sustainable success? It's about evolving your mindset, staying open to disruption and positioning yourself in environments where opportunity can strike. **Quantum leaps aren't the result of luck – they come from continuously expanding who you are** and what you're capable of handling.

BUILDING CAPACITY FOR SUSTAINABILITY

Achieving a quantum leap is thrilling but what's even more important is building the capacity to sustain that new level of success. Too often, leaders make a big breakthrough only to falter because they don't have the systems, resilience or mindset to handle the rapid change. **Sustainable success** isn't just about getting to the top, it's about staying there and continuing to grow.

Take **Amazon**, for example. After making its leap as an e-commerce giant, **Jeff Bezos** didn't rest on his laurels. He continued to invest in infrastructure – building warehouses, innovating logistics and expanding Amazon Web Services (AWS). This foresight allowed Amazon to scale rapidly without crumbling under its own weight.

To build capacity for sustainable success, focus on:

1. **Resilience**: Develop the emotional, mental and physical stamina to handle the increased demands that come with higher levels of success. This means managing stress, maintaining energy and staying adaptable. Like quantum particles adjusting to external forces, leaders must adapt to changing conditions without losing their momentum.

2. **Systems and processes**: Put structures in place that allow your business or team to function smoothly as it grows. Think about automation, delegation and operational efficiency — these systems free you up to focus on **big-picture strategy**.
3. **Continuous learning**: Stay curious and keep evolving. The strategies that got you here won't necessarily carry you forward. Be open to new ideas and flexible as you scale. Like quantum systems that constantly shift states, you must remain agile and ready to grow in response to new challenges and opportunities.

Sustaining success isn't just about **working harder,** it's about **working smarter**. By building the right foundation, you can continue to grow and thrive long after you've made your initial leap.

CHECKLIST FOR CHAPTER THIRTEEN: EXPANDING YOUR CAPACITY FOR SUCCESS

This chapter is about realising your potential for success and expanding beyond what you thought possible. It's not about small, incremental steps forward; it's about making those quantum leaps that propel you into new realms of possibility. Here's a checklist to help you expand your capacity for success and move beyond your limits:

Shift Your Mindset for Quantum Leaps

- **Believe in Nonlinear Growth:** Understand that success doesn't have to be incremental. Open yourself to the idea that massive breakthroughs can happen in an instant.
- **Challenge Conventional Thinking:** Rethink your approach to success. Instead of focusing on working harder, align your thoughts, energy and actions to create space for bigger leaps.
- **Adopt a Bold Mindset:** Ask yourself, "What bold action can I take today to disrupt my current limits?" Be willing to think differently and take unconventional steps.

Practice Disruptive Unlearning

- **Let Go of Old Success Models:** Identify methods or beliefs that have served you in the past but are now holding you back. Be willing to disrupt these patterns.
- **Ask Hard Questions:** Challenge your assumptions: "What beliefs am I holding onto that may limit my future growth?"
- **Make Room for Innovation:** Free yourself from outdated thinking so you can embrace new opportunities and innovative approaches.

Engineer Serendipity

- **Create Space for Unplanned Opportunities:** Look for environments where new ideas and chance encounters can lead to breakthroughs. Attend events, build diverse networks and step outside your usual routines.
- **Foster Collaboration:** Deliberately seek collaboration with people outside your industry or field of expertise. Innovation often happens when different perspectives collide.
- **Stay Open to the Unexpected:** Stay flexible and curious. Sometimes the biggest leaps come from opportunities you didn't plan for but were ready to seize.

Connect the Dots for Breakthroughs

- **Look for Patterns:** Practice seeing the connections between seemingly unrelated ideas. These links can spark new strategies and quantum leaps.
- **Hold Multiple Possibilities:** Like quantum particles that exist in multiple states at once, allow yourself to explore different ideas simultaneously without rushing to a single conclusion.
- **Embrace Uncertainty:** Be comfortable with not having all the answers immediately. Sometimes the path forward only becomes clear when you're open to exploring the unknown.

Build the Foundation for a Quantum Leap

- **Strengthen Your Mental and Emotional Resilience:** Just as athletes train for their biggest moments, build the stamina, focus and mindset needed to handle success when it arrives.
- **Lay the Groundwork:** Quantum leaps happen when you've put in the necessary prep work. Focus on alignment, strategy and readiness, so that when the opportunity arises, you're primed to take the leap.
- **Stay Open to Learning:** Constantly evolve your thinking. The strategies that got you to your current level won't necessarily take you to the next.

Leverage Serendipity for Sustainable Success

- **Create Environments for Serendipity:** Whether it's 20% time like Google's policy or fostering a culture of innovation, allow room for creative, unplanned ideas to take shape.
- **Turn Random Moments Into Strategy:** When chance encounters or new ideas come your way, practice connecting the dots and turning them into actionable, strategic breakthroughs.

Build Capacity for Sustainable Success

- **Develop Resilience:** Ensure you have the emotional, mental and physical stamina to handle increased demands as your success grows.
- **Establish Systems and Processes:** Put operational structures in place to support your growth, like delegating tasks, automating processes and refining systems to free up your time for strategic work.
- **Continue Learning and Evolving:** The journey doesn't stop with one quantum leap. Stay curious, adaptable and open to evolving as new challenges arise.

Maintain a Big-Picture Focus

- **Look Beyond Immediate Gains:** Ask yourself, "What long-term growth am I building towards? How can I position myself for sustainable success, not just one-off wins?"
- **Expand Your Capacity Over Time:** Focus on continual improvement, resilience and learning, ensuring that each quantum leap sets the stage for ongoing growth rather than burnout.

Reflect on Your Progress

- **Celebrate Quantum Leaps:** Recognise and celebrate when you make significant breakthroughs. This isn't just about small wins — it's about recognising the exponential shifts in your success.
- **Evaluate What's Next:** After a quantum leap, take time to reflect: "How do I continue to expand my capacity to handle even more success?"

14

LEADERSHIP LEGACY AND LASTING IMPACT

As we bring this journey to a close, there's a question that every leader must eventually confront: *When the spotlight dims and your career winds down, what will remain?* Will your legacy be defined by business wins, or will it stretch beyond profits, leaving an ethical mark that resonates for years to come?

The concept of legacy might seem distant, something for the final chapters of your career, but the truth is, your legacy is being crafted right now. Every decision you make, every value you stand by and every person you influence is shaping what you'll leave behind. It's not just about what people will say when you're no longer around — it's about the impact you have today and how it feels to live that impact authentically, both now and over time.

Building a meaningful legacy isn't about waiting until the end; it's about aligning your vision, values and beliefs with how you lead every single day. It's about living a life that feels good — not just in the immediate rush of success but as something sustainable and fulfilling over time. *Are you building the life and legacy that feel right to you?*

ALIGNING VISION, VALUES AND BELIEFS

The cornerstone of your legacy is living in alignment with your vision, values and beliefs. Your vision is the future you're striving to create — not just for your organisation, but for yourself and those you influence. Your values are the principles that guide you along that journey. Your beliefs are what you hold to be true about yourself, others and the world around you.

When you bring these three elements into alignment, you're not just chasing success, you're building a life that feels meaningful and intentional. Every decision becomes a reflection of who you are and what you stand for. This isn't just about achieving career milestones or financial wins; it's about how you lead, how you live and how you make others feel along the way.

Vision gives you direction. **Values** give you the framework to make decisions. **Beliefs** shape how you approach challenges and opportunities. Together, these are the foundations of your leadership legacy. When you live in alignment with these, you create a lasting impact that feels right — not just to others, but to you personally.

BUILDING YOUR LEADERSHIP LEGACY WITH INTENT

A legacy doesn't happen by accident, it's built intentionally through the choices you make today. The question is: *What do you want to be remembered for?* If you don't define your legacy, others will, and it may not reflect the true essence of who you are.

Your leadership legacy is constructed in the everyday moments — when you choose integrity over convenience, when you stand by your values in tough situations and when you inspire others by living authentically. *Are your daily decisions building the life and legacy you want?*

To truly define your legacy, you need to be intentional. Every decision, every action is an opportunity to reflect your vision and values. When you align these elements, you don't just create success, you create a life that feels good – one that stands the test of time.

LIVING YOUR VALUES EVERY DAY

Think back to the values that matter most to you. Maybe it's integrity, compassion, innovation or resilience. Whatever they are, these values shouldn't just be words on a page, they should be visible in how you live and lead. They should guide you in both the big strategic moves and the small everyday actions.

Take Nelson Mandela, for example. His legacy wasn't just about political victories, it was about living his values of forgiveness and reconciliation, even after years of imprisonment. He didn't just speak about reconciliation; he lived it by inviting his former jailer to his inauguration as president of South Africa. Mandela's values were at the core of every decision he made, shaping a legacy that still resonates today.

The lesson here is simple: *Living your values builds your legacy.* What you do when the pressure is on, when it's difficult to stand by your principles, defines who you are as a leader. Your leadership is about more than business success, it's about leading with values that guide your decisions and inspire others.

MENTORSHIP: EXTENDING YOUR LEGACY

Your legacy isn't only about the work you do; it's about the people you influence and inspire. Mentorship is one of the most powerful ways to extend your impact beyond your immediate circle and into future generations of leaders.

True mentorship isn't about giving advice, it's about helping others grow by living your values and sharing your journey authentically. When you mentor others, you plant the seeds for your legacy in the minds of the next generation. You shape how they lead, how they face challenges and how they pass on those lessons to others.

Who are you mentoring? Are you investing in the people around you, helping them develop not just skills but a sense of purpose, clarity and alignment with their vision and values? The more you invest in others, the more your legacy will ripple outward, creating a lasting impact.

VISION AND LEGACY: LIVING A LIFE THAT FEELS GOOD

At its core, your leadership legacy is about the kind of life you're building — not just professionally, but personally. Are you living a life that feels good to you, one that aligns with your vision of success, fulfilment and impact?

It's easy to get caught up in the pursuit of external achievements — titles, accolades and financial rewards — but true legacy is about more than that. It's about living in a way that feels meaningful. It's about making choices that resonate with your personal beliefs and that allow you to wake up each day knowing you're on the right path, not just in business but in life.

Success without personal alignment will eventually leave you feeling drained, disconnected and unfulfilled. But when you live and lead in alignment with your deepest values and vision, you create a sense of purpose that sustains you. *What does success mean to you?* How can you build a life that feels fulfilling now and will continue to feel that way over time?

ETHICAL DECISION-MAKING FOR LASTING IMPACT

Your leadership legacy isn't just defined by your vision and values, it's also shaped by the ethical decisions you make along the way. Ethics are where your values meet action, where your leadership is tested and proven.

For example, when Satya Nadella took over as CEO of Microsoft, he didn't just focus on business growth, he shifted the company's culture to one of empathy and inclusivity. This wasn't just about creating a profitable business; it was about leading ethically and making decisions that were grounded in his values of collaboration and fairness. Nadella's ethical leadership reshaped Microsoft's identity and will be a core part of his legacy.

Your ethical choices today are the foundation of your reputation, and the trust others place in you. They're the decisions that shape how people remember you, not just in business but in life. *Are you leading with ethics? Are you making decisions that align with your values, even when it's hard?*

THE RIPPLE EFFECT OF ETHICAL LEADERSHIP

The choices you make as a leader create ripples, affecting not just your immediate team but the broader world around you.

Take Yvon Chouinard, founder of Patagonia. His commitment to sustainability and ethical business practices set a new standard in the industry, proving that profitability and responsibility can coexist. Patagonia's long-term success isn't just financial, it's rooted in ethical decisions that reflect Chouinard's values.

Ethical leadership creates a ripple effect that extends far beyond your immediate impact. It inspires others to lead with integrity, to prioritise what's right over what's easy and to build a world where values matter as much as outcomes. *What kind of ripple effect are you creating with your leadership?*

LONG-TERM CONSEQUENCES OF UNETHICAL LEADERSHIP

While ethical leadership builds trust and lasting impact, unethical behaviour will eventually unravel any success you've built. Consider the collapse of Enron — once a celebrated company, now remembered as one of the biggest corporate scandals in history. The leaders of Enron may have had short-term gains, but their unethical decisions destroyed their legacy, their company and the lives of those who trusted them.

The takeaway is simple: *Your legacy is only as strong as your ethics.* No amount of success can cover up for unethical behaviour and when the cracks appear, the damage can be irreparable. Leading with integrity is the only way to ensure that your legacy stands the test of time.

LIVING YOUR LEGACY TODAY

As you reflect on your leadership, ask yourself: *Am I living in alignment with my vision, values, and beliefs?* Are your decisions, actions and relationships building the life and legacy you want to leave behind?

Remember, your leadership legacy isn't something you'll build in the future, it's something you're shaping right now. Every decision, every conversation, every challenge is an opportunity to create the legacy you want. It's about leading with purpose, living your values and ensuring that your success feels right — not just in the moment but in the long run.

What will your legacy be? More importantly, does it align with the life you want to live and the impact you want to leave behind?

When you lead with clarity, integrity and purpose, your legacy will be one that feels good not just to the world, but to you.

RESOURCES

The Resilient Leader Programme: is a transformative, on-demand audio solution tailored for high-performing leaders who need rapid and lasting relief from stress and performance blocks. Powered by the groundbreaking Quantum Release Method™, this programme directly addresses the root causes of stress by reprogramming the unconscious mind and regulating the nervous system. Unlike traditional methods, it eliminates stress and pressure at their core, delivering fast, tangible results without lengthy processes or revisiting painful memories.

1-2-1 Intensive Sessions: are 90-minute transformative experiences with an experienced Achievement Algorithm Practitioner. These sessions leverage the powerful Quantum Release Method™ to help you break through any stress, pressure, or performance blocks you're facing.

Tailored to your specific needs, these intensives are designed to deliver rapid, lasting results—allowing you to move through challenges with clarity, confidence, and ease. Whether you're dealing with personal hurdles or professional obstacles, our practitioners will guide you to overcome them and unlock your full potential.

Experience a shift like never before, and leave each session feeling lighter, more focused, and fully empowered to take on what's next.

Retainer Packages: offer ongoing support and access to experienced *Achievement Algorithm Practitioners* whenever you need it. Designed for leaders and high performers, these packages provide consistent, tailored guidance to help you stay clear, focused, and resilient through life's challenges.

With regular check-ins and on-demand sessions, you'll have a trusted resource to:

- Navigate high-pressure situations.
- Address stress, anxiety, or performance blocks as they arise.
- Strategically apply the *R.A.I.S.E Framework* to align your actions with your goals, ensuring maximum impact and clarity.
- Maintain alignment with your priorities and long-term vision.

Whether it's a quick mindset reset, strategic guidance, or deeper work to overcome obstacles, our retainer packages ensure you always have the support you need to lead and perform at your best. Flexible and adaptable, these packages are built around your unique needs, helping you apply the most effective strategies to thrive with confidence and ease.

FREE RESOURCES

The SHIFT IT Audio Tool: Simply press play and follow the guided instructions. The SHIFT IT tool is embedded with the transformative Quantum Release Method™, designed to reprogramme your subconscious mind. It works instantly to clear pressure, stress, and anxiety, helping you navigate any challenging situation with ease and clarity.

Podcast: The Achievement Algorithm Podcast delivers practical advice and transformative techniques to overcome stress, build resilience, and unlock your full potential. Whether you're looking to sharpen your focus, boost productivity, or lead with confidence, The Achievement Algorithm Podcast equips you with actionable steps to thrive in every area of your life and career. Tune in and start your journey towards sustained success and clarity today.

SOCIAL MEDIA:

https://www.instagram.com/achievementalgorithm/

https://www.linkedin.com/in/achivementalgorithm/

https://www.youtube.com/@achievementalgorithm

ABOUT THE AUTHOR

Charlotte Fuller, founder of the Achievement Algorithm, stands at the forefront of leadership and innovation, acclaimed as the number one woman in tech and startups for her pioneering contributions. Armed with a Master's in Leadership and trained in rapid methods for nervous system regulating, high performance optimisation and advanced methods for clearing blocks and removing the pressure that comes from high pressure situations.

As a former corporate executive, Charlotte has collaborated with leading organisations globally, harnessing her insight to drive transformative change and sustainable success. Her role as a peak performance mentor underscores her commitment to guiding individuals towards their highest potential, leveraging new, rapid transformation methods rooted in nervous system regulation.

Beyond her accolades and professional achievements, Charlotte Fuller is a trailblazer in leadership practices, advocating for an approach focused on peak performance. Her upcoming book, *The Achievement Algorithm,* promises to redefine leadership paradigms, offering a roadmap to true high performance and enduring success.

Website: https://achievementalgorithm.com/

Email: info@achievementalgorithm.com

REFERENCES

Albulescu, P., Macsinga, I., Rusu, A., Sulea, C., Bodnaru, A., & Tulbure, B. T. (2022). "Give me a break!" A systematic review and meta-analysis on the efficacy of micro-breaks for increasing well-being and performance. *PLOS ONE, 17*(8). https://doi.org/10.1371/journal.pone.0272460

American Psychological Association. (n.d.). *APA PsycNet*. Psycnet.apa.org. Retrieved October 14, 2024, from https://psycnet.apa.org/doiLanding?doi=10.1037%2F0022-3514.74.5.1252

Ariga, A., & Lleras, A. (2011). Brief and rare mental "breaks" keep you focused: deactivation and reactivation of task goals preempt vigilance decrements. *Cognition, 118*(3), 439–443. https://doi.org/10.1016/j.cognition.2010.12.007

Baer, R. A., Smith, G. T., & Allen, K. B. (2004). Assessment of Mindfulness by Self-Report. *Assessment, 11*(3), 191–206. https://doi.org/10.1177/1073191104268029

Beck, A. T. (1970). Cognitive therapy: Nature and relation to behavior therapy. *Behavior Therapy, 1*(2), 184–200. https://doi.org/10.1016/s0005-7894(70)80030-2

Beyer, R. (2022, January 28). *A Global Look at the Connections Between Happiness, Income, and Meaning*. Stanford Graduate School of Business. https://www.gsb.stanford.edu/insights/global-look-connections-between-happiness-income-meaning

Brown, K. W., & Ryan, R. M. (2003). *APA PsycNet*. Psycnet.apa.org. https://psycnet.apa.org/record/2003-02410-012

Cacciotti, G., Hayton, J. C., Mitchell, J. R., & Allen, D. G. (2020). Entrepreneurial fear of failure: Scale development and validation. *Journal of Business Venturing, 35*(5), 106041. https://doi.org/10.1016/j.jbusvent.2020.106041

Carl Buchheit, PhD. (2019, May 8). *The History of Early NLP - Carl Buchheit, PhD*. Carl Buchheit, PhD. https://www.carlbuchheitphd.com/articles/history-of-early-nlp/

Cascio, C. N., O'Donnell, M. B., Tinney, F. J., Lieberman, M. D., Taylor, S. E., Strecher, V. J., & Falk, E. B. (2015). Self-affirmation activates brain systems associated with self-related processing and reward and is reinforced by future orientation. *Social Cognitive and Affective Neuroscience, 11*(4), 621–629. https://doi.org/10.1093/scan/nsv136

Christensen, C. M. (1997). *The Innovator's Dilemma: When New Technologies Cause Great Firms to Fail*. Harvard Business School. https://www.hbs.edu/faculty/Pages/item.aspx?num=46

Cleveland Clinic. (2022). *Parasympathetic nervous system (PSNS): What it is & function*. Cleveland Clinic; Cleveland Clinic. https://my.clevelandclinic.org/health/body/23266-parasympathetic-nervous-system-psns

Colzato, L. S., Ozturk, A., & Hommel, B. (2012). Meditate to Create: The Impact of Focused-Attention and Open-Monitoring Training on Convergent and Divergent Thinking. *Frontiers in Psychology, 3*(116). https://doi.org/10.3389/fpsyg.2012.00116

Courtenay, M. de . (2024, June 4). *De-escalating with CALM - Performance Frontiers*. Performance Frontiers. https://performancefrontiers.com/thought-frontiers/insights/de-escalation-with-calm/

Csikszentmihalyi, M. (1990, January). *Flow: The Psychology of Optimal Experience*. ResearchGate; Harper & Row. https://www.researchgate.net/publication/224927532_Flow_The_Psychology_of_Optimal_Experience

Curran, T., & Hill, A. P. (2019). Perfectionism is increasing over time: A meta-analysis of birth cohort differences from 1989 to 2016. *Psychological Bulletin, 145*(4), 410–429. https://doi.org/10.1037/bul0000138

Davidson, R. J., & Lutz, A. (2008). Buddha's Brain: Neuroplasticity and Meditation. *IEEE Signal Processing Magazine, 25*(1), 176–174. https://www.ncbi.nlm.nih.gov/pmc/articles/PMC2944261/

de Looff, P. C., Cornet, L. J. M., Embregts, P. J. C. M., Nijman, H. L. I., & Didden, H. C. M. (2018). Associations of sympathetic and parasympathetic activity in job stress and burnout: A systematic review. *PLoS ONE, 13*(10). https://doi.org/10.1371/journal.pone.0205741

DE-ESCALATION SERIES FOR CRITICAL INFRASTRUCTURE OWNERS AND OPERATORS DE-ESCALATION " De-Escalation. (n.d.). Retrieved October 9, 2024, from https://www.cisa.gov/sites/default/files/publications/De-Escalation_Final%20508%20%2809.21.21%29.pdf

Dehghan Nayyeri, M., Burgmer, M., & Pfleiderer, B. (2019). Impact of pressure as a tactile stimulus on working memory in healthy participants. *PLOS ONE, 14*(3), e0213070. https://doi.org/10.1371/journal.pone.0213070

Din, U., & Zhang, L. (2023). Unveiling the mechanisms through which leader integrity shapes ethical leadership behavior: Theory of planned behavior perspective. *Behavioral Sciences, 13*(11), 928–928. https://doi.org/10.3390/bs13110928

Dweck, C. (2006). *Mindset: The new psychology of success*. Psycnet.apa.org. https://psycnet.apa.org/record/2006-08575-000

Fannin, J. L., & Williams, R. M. (n.d.). Leading-Edge Neuroscience Reveals Significant Correlations Between Beliefs, the Whole-Brain State, and Psychotherapy. In *https://psych-k.com/wp-content/uploads/2013/10/FanninWilliams.CQ-copy.pdf*. Retrieved September 4, 2020, from https://psych-k.com/wp-content/uploads/2013/10/FanninWilliams.CQ-copy.pdf

Finerman, A. (2019, November 19). *The Impact of Limiting Beliefs*. Wharton Magazine. https://magazine.wharton.upenn.edu/digital/the-impact-of-limiting-beliefs/

Franklin, B. A., Rusia, A., Haskin-Popp, C., & Tawney, A. (2021). Chronic Stress, Exercise and Cardiovascular Disease: Placing the Benefits and Risks of Physical Activity into Perspective. *International Journal of Environmental Research and Public Health, 18*(18), 9922. https://doi.org/10.3390/ijerph18189922

Frost, R. O., Marten, P., Lahart, C., & Rosenblate, R. (1990). The dimensions of perfectionism. *Cognitive Therapy and Research, 14*(5), 449–468. https://doi.org/10.1007/bf01172967

Global Leadership Forecast 2023. (n.d.). *Global Leadership Forecast 2023*. Retrieved October 19, 2024, from https://assets-us-01.kc-usercontent.com/469992e5-7cbd-0032-ead4-f2db9237053a/19c8dfff-4c5a-4c39-b046-f9bb074513d7/Global%20Leadership%20Forecast%202023.pdf

Knezevic, E., Katarina Nenic, Milanovic, V., & Nebojsa Nick Knezevic. (2023). The Role of Cortisol in Chronic Stress, Neurodegenerative Diseases, and Psychological Disorders. *Cells, 12*(23), 2726–2726. https://doi.org/10.3390/cells12232726

Kong, F., Zhao, L., & Tsai, C.-H. (2020). The Relationship Between Entrepreneurial Intention and Action: The Effects of Fear of Failure and Role Model. *Frontiers in Psychology, 11*. https://doi.org/10.3389/fpsyg.2020.00229

Kresser, C. (2019, May 17). *Sympathetic vs. Parasympathetic State: How Stress Affects Your Health*. Chris Kresser; chriskresser.com. https://chriskresser.com/sympathetic-vs-parasympathetic-state-how-stress-affects-your-health/

Laureiro-Martínez, D., & Brusoni, S. (2018). Cognitive flexibility and adaptive decision-making: Evidence from a laboratory study of expert decision-makers. *Strategic Management Journal, 39*(4), 1031–1058. https://doi.org/10.1002/smj.2774

Lazar, S. W., Kerr, C. E., Wasserman, R. H., Gray, J. R., Greve, D. N., Treadway, M. T., McGarvey, M., Quinn, B. T., Dusek, J. A., Benson, H., Rauch, S. L., Moore, C. I., & Fischl, B. (2005). Meditation experience is associated with increased cortical thickness. *Neuroreport, 16*(17), 1893–1897. https://www.ncbi.nlm.nih.gov/pmc/articles/PMC1361002/

Leroy, S. (2009). Why is it so hard to do my work? The challenge of attention residue when switching between work tasks. *Organizational Behavior and Human Decision Processes, 109*(2), 168–181. https://doi.org/10.1016/j.obhdp.2009.04.002

Maria Cecilia Henriquez-Daza, Joan-Lluís Capelleras, & Osorio-Tinoco, F. (2023). *Does fear of failure affect entrepreneurial growth aspirations? The moderating role of institutional collectivism in emerging and developed countries*. https://doi.org/10.1108/jeee-08-2022-0232

Mayer, J. D., Salovey, P., & Caruso, D. R. (2004). Emotional intelligence: Theory, findings, and implications. *Psychological Inquiry, 15*(3), 197–215. https://doi.org/10.1207/s15327965pli1503_02

Mayo Clinic. (2021, July 8). *Chronic stress puts your health at risk*. Mayo Clinic; Mayo Foundation for Medical Education and Research. https://www.mayoclinic.org/healthy-lifestyle/stress-management/in-depth/stress/art-20046037

Naser, M. J., Hasan, N. E., Zainaldeen, M. H., Zaidi, A., Mohamed, Y. M. A. M. H., & Fredericks, S. (2022). Impostor Phenomenon and Its Relationship to Self-Esteem Among Students at an International Medical College in the Middle East: A Cross-Sectional Study. *Frontiers in Medicine, 9*(850434). https://doi.org/10.3389/fmed.2022.850434

Nayar, V. (2013, February 18). *The Power of Intent.* Harvard Business Review. https://hbr.org/2013/02/the-power-of-intent

NeuroLaunch editorial team. (2024a, September 22). *De-escalating Aggressive Behavior: Effective Techniques for Defusing Tense Situations.* NeuroLaunch.com. https://neurolaunch.com/how-to-de-escalate-aggressive-behavior/

NeuroLaunch editorial team. (2024b, September 30). *Somatic Intelligence: Harnessing the Body's Wisdom for Enhanced Well-being.* NeuroLaunch.com. https://neurolaunch.com/somatic-intelligence/

Nutley, T. (2023, February 3). *NLP Anchoring: A Comprehensive Guide.* UKCPD. https://ukcpd.co.uk/nlp-anchoring-a-comprehensive-guide/

Odot, L. (2023, November 2). *Case study: how Shell anticipated the 1973 oil crisis.* Polytechnique Insights. https://www.polytechnique-insights.com/en/columns/society/case-study-how-shell-anticipated-the-1973-oil-crisis/

Patrick, V. M., & Hagtvedt, H. (2012). "I Don't" versus "I Can't": When Empowered Refusal Motivates Goal-Directed Behavior. *Journal of Consumer Research, 39*(2), 371–381. https://doi.org/10.1086/663212

Price, C. J., & Weng, H. Y. (2021). Facilitating Adaptive Emotion Processing and Somatic Reappraisal via Sustained Mindful Interoceptive Attention. *Frontiers in Psychology, 12*. https://doi.org/10.3389/fpsyg.2021.578827

Rē Precision Health. (2024, August). *Sympathetic Dominance - The Result Of Chronic Stress*. Rē Precision Health. https://www.reprecisionhealth.com/resources/sympathetic-dominance

Reynolds, E. (2023, September 19). *Gimme a (micro)break!* BPS. https://www.bps.org.uk/research-digest/gimme-microbreak

Rohrbeck, R., & Schwarz, J. O. (2013). The value contribution of strategic foresight: Insights from an empirical study of large European companies. *Technological Forecasting and Social Change, 80*(8), 1593–1606. https://doi.org/10.1016/j.techfore.2013.01.004

S, M., S, O., & P, S. (2002, May 1). *Combining Motivational and Volitional Interventions to Promote Exercise Participation: Protection Motivation Theory and Implementation Intentions*. British Journal of Health Psychology. https://pubmed.ncbi.nlm.nih.gov/14596707/

Savic, I., Perski, A., & Osika, W. (2017). MRI Shows that Exhaustion Syndrome Due to Chronic Occupational Stress is Associated with Partially Reversible Cerebral Changes. *Cerebral Cortex, 28*(3), 894–906. https://doi.org/10.1093/cercor/bhw413

Sawada, T., Hiroki Okawara, Nakashima, D., Iwabuchi, S., Matsumoto, M., Nakamura, M., & Takeo Nagura. (2022). Effects of alternating heat and cold stimulation at different cooling rates using a wearable thermo device on shoulder muscle stiffness: a cross-over study. *BMC Musculoskeletal Disorders, 23*(1). https://doi.org/10.1186/s12891-022-05623-z

Sawada, T., Okawara, H., Nakashima, D., Aoki, K., Namba, M., Iwabuchi, S., Katsumata, Y., Nakamura, M., & Nagura, T. (2024). Local alternating heat and cold stimulation affects hemodynamics and oxygenation in fatigued muscle tissue and autonomic nervous activity: a single-arm interventional study. *Journal of Physiological Anthropology, 43*(1). https://doi.org/10.1186/s40101-024-00358-3

Scoblic, P. (2020, July 1). *Learning from the Future.* Harvard Business Review. https://hbr.org/2020/07/learning-from-the-future

Shane, Ph.D., LMT, P. (2014). *Somatic Maps of Emotional Body Experiences | The Center for Bodymind Education.* Centerforbodymindeducation.com. https://centerforbodymindeducation.com/somatic-maps-of-emotional-body-experiences/

Shao, J., Chen, Y., Gao, D., Liu, Y., Hu, N., Yin, L., Zhang, X., & Yang, F. (2023). Ventromedial hypothalamus relays chronic stress inputs and exerts bidirectional regulation on anxiety state and related sympathetic activity. *Frontiers in Cellular Neuroscience, 17.* https://doi.org/10.3389/fncel.2023.1281919

T. Franklin Murphy. (2023, December 16). *Somatic Markers*. Psychology Fanatic. https://psychologyfanatic.com/somatic-markers/

The Serendipity Mindset. (n.d.). *The Serendipity Mindset – By Christian Busch, PhD*. The Serendipity Mindset. Retrieved October 15, 2024, from https://theserendipitymindset.com/

Thomas, J. (2020, May 6). *Decisions, Decisions, Decisions – Is the Concept of Decision Fatigue an Issue in Covid-19 Times? By Rita Symons – The official blog of BMJ Leader*. Bmj.com. https://blogs.bmj.com/bmjleader/2020/05/06/decisions-decisions-decisions-is-the-concept-of-decision-fatigue-an-issue-in-covid-19-times-by-rita-symons/

World Health Organization. (2019). *Burn-out an "occupational phenomenon": International classification of diseases*. World Health Organization. https://www.who.int/news/item/28-05-2019-burn-out-an-occupational-phenomenon-international-classification-of-diseases

Printed in Great Britain
by Amazon

56593291R00121